W|D

DATE DUE

The
Miniature
Pinscher

An Owner's Guide To

A HAPPY HEALTHY PET

Howell Book House

Howell Book House

A Simon & Schuster Macmillan Company
1633 Broadway
New York, NY 10019-6785

Macmillan Publishing books may be purchased for business or sales promotional use. For information please write: Special Markets Department, Macmillan Publishing USA, 1633 Broadway, New York, NY 10019-6785.

MACMILLAN is a registered trademark of Macmillan, Inc.

Library of Congress Cataloging-in-Publication Data
Radel, Rose J.
    The miniature pinscher / [Rose J. Radel].
       p.   cm. — (An owner's guide to a happy healthy pet)
    Includes bibliographical references (p.).
    ISBN 0-87605-229-4
    1. Miniature pinscher. I. Title. II. Series.
  SF429.M56R335   1998
  636.76—dc21   98-37225
                    CIP

Manufactured in the United States of America

10 9 8 7 6 5 4 3 2 1

Series Director: Amanda Pisani
Series Assistant Director: Jennifer Liberts
Book Design: Michele Laseau
Cover Design: Iris Jeromnimon
Illustrations: Shelley Norris and Jeff Yesh
Photography:
   Front cover by Paulette Braun and back cover by Bob Schwartz
   American Kennel Club: 18
   Paulette Braun: i, 2–3, 19
   Kristi Hart: 50, 53, 78
   Cheryl Primeau: 36, 58, 59
   Rose J. Radel: 5, 6, 8, 9, 10, 12, 14, 16, 20, 27, 28, 31, 38, 40, 42, 45, 47, 61,
      63, 64, 88
   Bob Schwartz: 15, 21, 54, 57
   Judith E. Strom: 22, 75
   Toni Tucker: 26, 62, 69
Production Team: Carrie Allen, Toi Davis, Clint Lahnen, Kristi Hart, Dennis Sheehan, Terri Sheehan

Contents

Welcome
to the
World

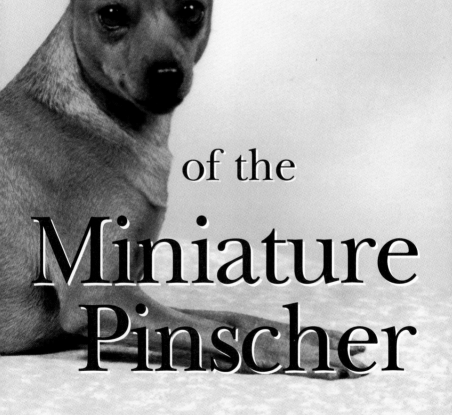

of the

Miniature Pinscher

External Features of the Miniature Pinscher

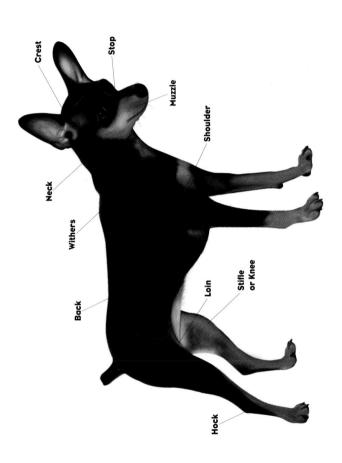

- Crest
- Stop
- Muzzle
- Shoulder
- Neck
- Withers
- Loin
- Stifle or Knee
- Back
- Hock

chapter 1

What Is a **Miniature Pinscher?**

The "King of Toys" moniker accurately describes the Mini-ature Pinscher. This proud breed possesses aregal presence which denotes a "here I am—look at me" attitude. Miniature Pinschers are naturally well groomed, spirited and vigorous. They are distinguished from other toy dogs by their distinctive gait, animation, boundless energy and complete self-possession.

"Min Pins," as they are affectionately called, are superb pets. They are adaptable and do well in most environments—be it a city apartment, suburban home or a farm. They are great all-around family dogs and want only to be with their human owners; and the fact that they are easy to groom, shed minimally, are very trainable and are good eaters makes them a breed made for today's busy lifestyles.

Despite their small size, Min Pins are excellent watch dogs. They quickly sound their vocal "alarms" to intruders and are fearless in the protection of their families. For this reason, they score well on the "temperament test" exercise in dog eventing, which requires the dog to stand his ground in protecting his handler. Though in the dog fancy of the United States they are classified and shown in the Toy group of dogs, in many countries they are grouped in the Guard group or, as in the case in Japan, the Working group.

A Big Dog in a Small Package

Many people think that the Miniature Pinscher is a "bred-down" version of the Doberman Pinscher. Nothing could be further from the truth—although the two breeds look alike, they are not related. Min Pins actually preceded Dober-mans by many years.

Most Miniature Pinschers are totally unaware of their diminutive size and will challenge much larger dogs. Though many large dogs are confused and startled by this fearless bravery from such a small source, a Min Pin owner must be alert to this tendency in order to avoid potentially dangerous skirmishes.

Despite the Min Pin's resemblance to the Doberman Pinscher, the two breeds are not related.

The breed is growing rapidly in popularity. At the end of 1997, Miniature Pinschers ranked 18th in the American Kennel Club's registry. This is easy to understand considering the breed's vibrant personality, keen intelligence and versatility. You may want to own a Min Pin, but you'll find that over time the Min Pin will own you—and you'll be glad for it. Your dog will provide you with warm companionship, constant amusement and a love and devotion unique to this wonderful breed.

The Breed Standard

While the perfect dog has yet to be born, each breed has an official standard that conscientious breeders strive to achieve. A Miniature Pinscher is a dog with a very balanced body. The Min Pin is well proportioned and with every body part blended in harmony. While beauty is in the eye of the beholder, few will disagree that the Min Pin form is very eye pleasing.

The Official Breed Standard

In the following discussion of the Miniature Pinscher Standard, the official standard is given in italics, and the author's commentary appears below it.

General Appearance *The Miniature Pinscher is structurally a well balanced, sturdy, compact, short-coupled, smooth-coated dog. He naturally is well groomed, proud, vigorous and alert. Characteristic traits are his hackney-like action, fearless animation, complete self-possession, and his spirited presence.*

> **WHAT IS A BREED STANDARD?**
>
> A breed standard—a detailed description of an individual breed—is meant to portray the ideal specimen of that breed. This includes ideal structure, temperament, gait, type—all aspects of the dog. Because the standard describes on ideal specimen, it isn't based on any particular dog. It is a concept against which judges compare actual dogs and breeders, strive to produce dogs. At a dog show, the dog that wins is the one that comes closest, in the judge's opinion, to the standard for its breed. Breed standards are written by the breed parent clubs, the national organizations formed to oversee the well-being of the breed. They are voted on and approved by the members of the parent clubs.

Size, Proportion, Substance Size—*10 inches to 12½ inches in height allowed, with desired height 11 inches to 11½ inches measured at highest point of the shoulder blades.* Disqualification—*Under 10 inches or over 12½ inches in height. Length of males equals height at withers. Females may be slightly longer.*

A Miniature Pinscher should be a square dog. This means that the distance from the withers (top of the shoulders) to the base of the tail, from the withers to the ground, and from the base of the tail to the ground, should form an invisible square. Dogs must measure between 10 and 12½ inches at the withers to be shown in "conformation" (where dogs are judged on how closely they conform to the standard and can become champions).

Breeders are constantly trying to breed the "perfect dog." At a dog show, such as the one pictured here, breeders' dogs are judged on how closely they conform to the breed standard.

Head *In correct proportion to the body. Tapering, narrow with well fitted but not too prominent foreface which balances with the skull. No indication of coarseness.* Eyes *full, slightly oval, clear, bright and dark even to a true black, including eye rims, with the exception of chocolates, whose eye rims should be self-colored.* Ears *set high, standing erect from base to tip. May be cropped or uncropped.*

Skull *appears flat, tapering forward toward the muzzle.* Muzzle *strong rather than fine and delicate, and in proportion to the head as a whole.* Head *well balanced with only a slight drop to the muzzle, which is parallel to the top of the skull.* Nose *black only, with the exception of chocolates which should have a self-colored nose.* Lips and Cheeks *small, taut and closely adherent to each other.* Teeth *meet in a scissors bite.*

A good Min Pin head denotes elegance and is sometimes referred to as "serpentine." It should be narrow, and the sides or cheeks should be flat rather than padded. The eyes should not be round or bulging but oval, dark, and set well into the head. The top teeth should close nicely over the lower to form a scissors bite. A level bite (top and lower teeth meet directly together), overshot bite (top teeth are too far over the lower) or undershot bite (lower teeth extend out under the top) are not desirable. Fanciers abroad place great emphasis on the bite and a complete set of teeth.

Until recent years, almost all Min Pins had cropped or cut ears. Cropping is normally done when a puppy is several weeks old. Because the procedure is performed under anesthesia, is costly, is cosmetic surgery and requires taping and postsurgical care, some owners prefer to leave the ears natural. In the United States, the ears must be erect, whether cropped or not, for a dog to be shown. In many other countries, they can be folded down or be erect. Cropping has not been permitted for decades in Great Britain, Australia and Africa.

Though ear cropping is still permitted in the United States, leaving the ears natural is just as acceptable, and many owners decide not to crop.

Neck, Topline, Body Neck *proportioned to head and body, slightly arched, gracefully curved, blending into shoulders, muscular and free from suggestion of dewlap or throatiness.* Topline *back level or slightly sloping toward the rear both when standing and gaiting.* Body *compact, slightly wedge-shaped, muscular.* Forechest *well developed.* Well sprung *ribs. Depth of brisket, the base line of which is level with points of the elbows. Belly moderately tucked up to denote grace of structural form. Short and strong in* loin. Croup *level with topline.* Tail *set high, held erect, docked in proportion to size of dog.*

Here, the standard adequately describes the neck and topline. The topline in profile should not be uneven or rise toward the rear.

In the description of the body, "well-sprung ribs" means that the ribs are rounded out. The brisket is the lower part of the chest, and the ideal depth would be for the lower chest to meet the elbows in profile.

The loin is the region on either side of the spinal column between the last rib and the hindquarters. The croup is the back of the rear at which the tail is set.

Rarely are tails not docked or cut on a Min Pin. Usually this is done when the puppy is a few days old and before the nervous system is fully developed. Therefore, it is relatively painless. The standard calls for the tail to be in proportion to the size of the dog. There is some variation in length based on breeder preference but usually not a great deal.

The tail should be carried vertically or at a slight angle, but still upward. A horizontal tail carriage is not desirable and can mean that the dog isn't happy.

Most owners have their Miniature Pinscher's tail docked.

Forequarters Shoulders *clean and sloping with moderate angulation coordinated to permit the hackney-like action.* Elbows *close to the body.* Legs *strong bone development and small clean joints. As viewed from the front, straight and upstanding.* Pasterns *strong, perpendicular.* Dewclaws *should be removed.* Feet *small, catlike, toes strong, well arched and closely knit with deep pads.* Nails *thick, blunt.*

The hackney-like action is a high lifting of the front legs with a slight bend at the wrist. This motion is similar to that of a hackney pony.

The pastern consists of the bones forming the joint directly above the foot. Dogs with weak pasterns are sometimes referred to as being "down in pastern." Diet and other conditions can cause this problem, and at times it can be remedied.

The dewclaws are the extra nails up from the foot on the inner leg. Because dewclaws serve no useful purpose and can catch on fences, bedding, clothing or any number of other hazards, they are usually removed when the tail is docked.

Hindquarters *Well muscled quarters set wide enough apart to fit into a properly balanced body. As viewed from the rear, the* legs *are straight and parallel. From the side, well angulated.* Thighs *well muscled.* Stifles *well-defined.* Hocks *short, set well apart.* Dewclaws *should be removed.* Feet *small, catlike, toes strong, well arched and closely knit with deep pads.* Nails *thick, blunt.*

"Well angulated" refers to the angle of the thigh. Ideally, the rear legs should resemble a sickle—be curved at the thigh with the hock (lower part of leg), straight and perpendicular to the ground.

Coat *Smooth, hard and short, straight and lustrous, closely adhering to and uniformly covering the body.*

The coat of a Min Pin should be sleek. A healthy dog's coat glistens, sheds little and requires minimal care. Suggestions on coat maintenance will be made in chapter 6.

Color *Solid clear red. Stag red (red with intermingling of black hairs). Black with sharply defined rust-red markings on cheeks, lips, lower jaw, throat, twin spots above eyes and chest, lower half of forelegs, inside of hind legs and vent region, lower portion of hocks and feet. Black pencil stripes on toes. Chocolate with rust-red markings the same as specified for blacks, except brown pencil stripes on toes. In the solid red and stag red a rich vibrant medium to dark shade is preferred.* Disqualifications—*Any color other than listed. Thumb mark (patch of black hair surrounded by rust on the front of the foreleg between the foot and the wrist; on chocolates, the patch is chocolate hair). White on any part of dog which exceeds one-half inch in its longest dimension.*

The majority of dogs that are shown today are red, but pet owners seem to prefer the black and rusts, perhaps because they more closely resemble the Doberman. Chocolate and rusts are rare and are more costly.

Any color not specified is not recognized by the American Kennel Club. While a dog with color

> ### THE AMERICAN KENNEL CLUB
>
> Familiarly referred to as "the AKC," the American Kennel Club is a nonprofit organization devoted to the advancement of purebred dogs. The AKC maintains a registry of recognized breeds and adopts and enforces rules for dog events including shows, obedience trials, field trials, hunting tests, lure coursing, herding, earthdog trials, agility and the Canine Good Citizen program. It is a club of clubs, established in 1884 and composed, today, of over 500 autonomous dog clubs throughout the United States. Each club is represented by a delegate; the delegates make up the legislative body of the AKC, voting on rules and electing directors. The American Kennel Club maintains the Stud Book, the record of every dog ever registered with the AKC, and publishes a variety of materials on purebred dogs, including a monthly magazine, books and numerous educational pamphlets. For more information, contact the AKC at the address listed in Chapter 13, "Resources," and look for the names of their publications in Chapter 12, "Recommended Reading."

Welcome to
the World of
the Miniature
Pinscher

*Everything from
the correct pro-
portions to a
healthy coat are
part of a properly
conformed dog.*

disqualifications cannot be shown in conformation, it can make a wonderful pet. It should not, however, be bred. Though they are not recognized in the United States, blue and rust dogs are recognized in Great Britain, Canada and elsewhere.

Gait *The forelegs and hind legs move parallel, with feet turning neither in nor out. The hackney-like action is a high-stepping, reaching, free and easy gait in which the front leg moves straight forward and in front of the body and the foot bends at the wrist. The dog drives smoothly and strongly from the rear. The head and tail are carried high.*

The hackney-like movement of a Min Pin distinguishes it from other toy dogs. Originally, the standard called for a "precise hackney gait," but in 1980, because this definition was not totally accurate, the standard was altered to describe the gait as "hackney-like action."

Temperament *Fearless anima-tion, complete self-possession, and spirited presence.*

The Min Pin temperament makes him an outstanding show dog, a good watch dog and a joy to observe at work or play. The owner who is consistent, firm and kind will reap the reward of an enjoyable member of the household.

Disqualifications *Under 10 inches or over 12½ inches in height.*

Any color other than listed. Thumb mark (patch of black hair surrounded by rust on the front of the foreleg between the foot and wrist; on chocolates, the patch is chocolate hair). White on any part of dog which exceeds one-half (½) inch in its longest dimension.

In addition to the breed disqualifications, there are general disqualifications specified by the American Kennel Club that apply to all breeds. Such disqualifications

12

include dogs that are deaf or blind, vicious or surgically altered (except for docking and cropping) and males that do not have both testicles descended into the scrotum.

These types of disqualifications, however, don't prevent a dog from being a great companion.

chapter 2

The
Miniature
Pinscher's
Ancestry

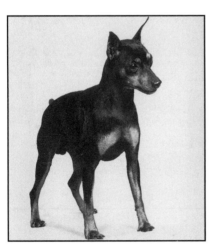

The origin of the Miniature Pinscher is veiled in obscurity. Archaeologists have found canine skeletons of very small dogs dating back to the Stone Age. Little dogs that resemble Min Pins have been in existence for several hundred years. While they looked quite different then, dogs similar to Miniature Pinschers have appeared in paintings and sculptures by the old masters centuries ago.

As stated earlier, the Miniature and Doberman Pinschers are two separate and distinct breeds. The Doberman Pinscher is named for Herr Karl Friedrich Louis Dobermann who is credited with producing the breed. His objective was to create a giant version of the then five-pound Reh Pinscher to serve as a guard dog. It is believed that the

German Shepherd and the Rottweiler were used for the Doberman initially. Some say Herr Dobermann crossed a Thuringia Shepherd with the medium-sized German Pinscher. Later, other breeds like the Standard Manchester Terrier and the Greyhound were thought to have been introduced to the breeding program.

Herr Dobermann's goal was to develop a medium-sized dog of intelligence and stamina requiring low maintenance to assist him in his work as a tax collector. By 1890 he bred a specimen that satisfied his intent. The German Pinscher Klub of Germany was formed in 1912. Miniature Pinschers were well established long before that time.

The History of the Min Pin

Breed historians agree that Min Pins were developed in Germany. Most claim that they descended from the Dachshund and the Italian Greyhound, both of which are breeds that have been in existence for ages. The German writer, Dr. H. G. Reinchenback made this claim as early as 1836.

It is believed that the Miniature Pinscher is descended from the Dachshund and the Italian Greyhound.

It is generally believed that the breed's colors were inherited from the Dachshund, its longer legs and elegance from the Italian Greyhound. Some claim that the old English Black and Tan Terriers are in the breed's background; still others believe they were bred down from the older German or Moyen Pinscher, a medium-sized look-alike. The Pug and Manchester Terrier have also been implicated in the breed's beginnings, but this is doubted by many. A cross between the Dachshund and Italian Greyhound could well produce just such a breed as the Miniature Pinscher, and both the Dachshund and the Italian Greyhound are very ancient breeds.

There are no factual documents to accurately support these various assumptions, so we can only speculate on the ancestry of the breed. Although its source is uncertain, the Min Pin of today attests to years of careful breeding which has refined and produced the current day's grace and elegance for which this breed is known.

The years during World War I were hard for the breed. Although Min Pins were extremely popular, irresponsible breeding sent the breed into a downward spiral.

THE MINIATURE PINSCHER AS A SHOW DOG

Dog shows began in Germany in 1863. The first German dog magazine, named simply *The Dog*, was published in 1876. Miniature Pinschers were officially recognized in Germany in 1880. They were first named Reh Pinschers because they resembled a very small species of deer, the Reh, that roamed the Black Forests of Germany. In the 1870s they were also sometimes referred to as Edelpinscher meaning Noble Pinscher. This legacy of a regal association dates back to the breed's early years and has remained a distinguishing earmark to this day.

GOLDEN ERAS AND TOUGH TIMES

The early 1900s were a golden era for the Reh Pinscher, and they were in high favor. The dogs were healthy, had good temperaments and were of excellent quality in conformation.

During World War I, however, the breed suffered a setback. Because of limited food rations, large dogs were difficult to maintain, and smaller dogs gained popularity. More Minia-ture Pinschers were bred and, as so often occurs when large numbers of dogs are produced in a short period, quality deteriorated.

After the war, due to the efforts of concerned breeders, the breed was quickly restored to its fine attributes—sturdy and healthy dogs in mind and body, small but full of fire and spirit. By the mid-1920s Min Pins were again flourishing. Miniature Pinschers, primarily from Western Germany, were exported to many countries but in greatest number to the United States.

THE MINIATURE PINSCHER IN AMERICA

During the 1920s, the breed gained popularity ra-pidly in the United States. The first Miniature Pinscher was registered with the American Kennel Club in 1925. In the late 1920s, Min Pins were shown in the Miscellaneous Class at dog shows, but only a limited number were exhibited. The breed was officially recog-nized by the American Kennel Club in 1929, with the formation of the Miniature Pinscher Club of America. A growth in the popularity of the breed followed.

Numerous breeders and kennels have produced outstanding Miniature Pinschers in the States over the years. It would be difficult to single out just several who have substantially contributed to the breed's success and influenced the fine quality that exists today.

THE BREED IN ENGLAND

The Miniature Pinscher Club in Britain is said to be a close-knit, friendly group of members who convene once a month. They hold their annual shows in central England so that most of their members can easily attend.

FAMOUS OWNERS OF THE MINIATURE PINSCHER

Veronica "Rocky" Cooper, wife of Gary Cooper

Charles "Lucky" Luciano

Demi Moore

Helen Chrysler Green

The advent of the breed in England is credited to Lionel Hamilton-Renwick who introduced the Miniature Pinscher to his country. I had the pleasure of meeting this fine gentleman in Monte Carlo, and we talked Miniature Pinschers for hours. His interest in the breed dates back many decades to when he first saw them in Switzerland. World War II delayed his plans for bringing Miniature Pinschers into his kennel in England.

Though this dog, a breed champion in 1946, looks similar to today's Min Pins, the difference between them can be noticed in his heavier build.

Following the war, in 1949 Hamilton-Renwick traveled over Europe to various kennels looking for good foundation stock. He succeeded in establishing the fine Birling line and had many outstanding winners with excellent progeny.

By 1960 various breeders in England imported Min Pins from the European continent and from the United States. At first, British Miniature Pinschers had drop ears. Eventually, the breeders strove for small erect ears and were successful. Cropping had been outlawed in Great Britain at the start of the century, so ears could not be surgically fixed. The English standard also specifies a "precise" hackney gait, whereas the American standard was ultimately amended to call for a "hackney-like action." Still, they found the best hackney gait was found primarily in American imports.

History tells us that the first Miniature Pinschers to be shown at the Crufts show were exhibited in 1956. The breed is consequently much newer to England than Germany, the United States and other parts of the globe.

THE BREED THROUGHOUT THE WORLD

Canada, Australia, New Zealand, Africa, Israel, France and Italy all have a significant number of breed fanciers. Some of these countries also have active Miniature Pinscher Clubs. In France, as in Germany, the breed is now combined with Schnauzers, and The Schnauzer-Pinscher Club of France has a huge following.

Miniature Pinscher Fanciers

Miniature Pinschers have fanciers the world over. In Europe, they are often seen being walked on the streets and in stores, restaurants and even on buses for which owners pay a reduced fare. (Dogs are permitted in most public places throughout Europe.)

Miniature Pinschers are loved around the world.

The breed has been owned and is favored by a number of prominent individuals. Princess Antoinette, President of the Monaco Kennel Club, has long had and admired the breed. At the annual show of the Monaco Kennel Club, her highness offers trophies for the Best of Breed winner. Our dogs have been honored with three of these, one for each year that we have competed there. In 1977, our trophy was presented to us by Princess Stephanie, then a child. The entire royal family usually attends final judging at their annual show.

Princess Antoinette has also donated breed trophies on occasion to the Empire Miniature Pinscher Club of Greater New York for their specialty show in New York City. The Princess is a most gracious lady and a devoted animal lover.

Mrs. Gary Cooper was the proud owner of Miniature Pinschers for many years. A lovely photo of Veronica "Rocky" Cooper and her Min Pin once appeared in the *New York Times*. I had the pleasure of meeting Rocky and one of her dogs at the Progressive Toy Dog Club Specialty in New York City at which her Min Pin was exhibited.

Helen Chrysler Greene, daughter of Walter Chrysler, the founder of Chrysler Motors, is a Miniature Pinscher breeder and active ex-hibitor. Her Dynasty Kennels have produced many champions and top-winning Miniature Pinschers over the years.

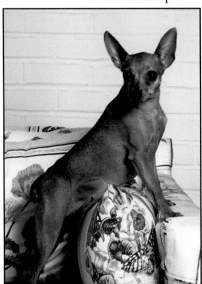

Because of the breed's elegance and regality, it has been the breed of choice for many famous (and infamous) characters.

One of the Andrew Sisters, the famed vocal group of the 1940s, was featured in a gourmet cookbook for dogs holding her black and rust pet.

Charles "Lucky" Luciano, Crime Syndicate Chief in New York City, once had a photograph published where he was reading a newspaper with his Miniature Pinscher perched on his neck and shoulder.

Actress Demi Moore was pictured on the cover of the *Ladies' Home Journal* in October 1995 holding her tiny Min Pin and a Yorkshire Terrier. An article on Ms. Moore was in-cluded in that issue, and the author referred to the fact that Demi held the Min Pin while being interviewed.

chapter 3

The **World**
According to the
Miniature
Pinscher

More so than with any other breed, I've heard people say that when they first saw a Miniature Pinscher, they knew someday they would own one. It's "love at first sight," if you will. The combination of that spirited presence and regal bearing can indeed be captivating. If you are attracted to small dogs with an attitude, and if you like a pet with minimal maintenance, the Min Pin is an excellent choice.

When you are in a somber mood, your dog will sense it. Being the characters that they are, your Min Pin will do all he can to lift your spirits—if only with a loving look. He can often make you smile and add zest to your day.

Miniature Pinschers are versatile and intelligent. They are adaptable to change and travel very well. The breed enjoys mental stimulation, and therefore responds well to training. Min Pins learn tricks easily, work well in Obedience and Agility (both American Kennel Club Events), score favorably on Temperament Tests, are good "hearing ear" and assistance dogs and are great actors and professional models. One of ours, Skippy, appeared on an episode of the TV show *New York Undercover,* and we've also worked several Min Pins with fashion models for magazine ads.

Character Traits
THE HUNTING INSTINCT

Originally, Miniature Pinschers were bred to be hunters. Farmers kept them on their property to control vermin. Though small in stature, they are a hearty dog and extremely swift. The hunting instinct is still

present in the Min Pin breed and, should they encounter them, Min Pins love to chase (and sometimes capture) squirrels, moles, mice, rats or other rodents.

The instinct to hunt rodents—the instinct that it was bred for—remains strong in the breed. Rab-

The Min Pin is a great contender in events such as Agility.

bits, squirrels and stray cats are fair game to your dog. Birds seem to only mildly interest Min Pins (wild birds will continue to eat from feeders even with the dogs nearby). On one occasion, one of our dogs didn't respond quickly when called to come in. We found him dragging a rabbit by the neck that weighed almost as much as he did. Fortunately, a sharp "no" made him drop the rabbit, which quickly hopped away. Rainier was left totally puzzled by our lack of enthusiasm for his prize capture.

Min Pins do best when they are mentally stimula-ted. They are a breed that loves to perform, truly eating up the attention. The Miniature Pinscher wants only to be with people. It is not a breed that can be content living outdoors or in a basement. They are social animals and want to be with their family. Min Pins require, if not demand, attention. They command the limelight wherever they go—be it strutting in the show ring, being walked down the street or being cuddled in the arms of someone who loves them. They love an audience and tend to know when they are the center of activity. They are born "hams."

The breed is also capable of learning to help out in the community. One of our dogs passed the test to become a certified Therapy Dog. This means that he is quali-fied to visit hospitals, nursing homes and similar facilities to cheer up patients. A male Min Pin that was sired by one of ours was used for drug detection work by a police force in Texas.

Min Pins are also a breed born to play and should have some structured time to do so every day. Some like to retrieve a ball or stick; others wrestle with you over a toy. They love to run, jump and bark. Min Pins will be willing part-ners for any game you can de-vise, and they rarely seem to tire of play.

A DOG'S SENSES

Sight: With their eyes located far-ther apart than ours, dogs can de-tect movement at a greater dis-tance than we can, but they can't see as well up close. They can also see better in less light, but they can't distinguish many colors.

Sound: Dogs can hear about four times better than we can, and they can hear high-pitched sounds especially well. Their ancestors, the wolves, howled to let other wolves know where they were; our dogs do the same, but they have a wider range of vocalizations, including barks, whimpers, moans and whines.

Smell: A dog's nose is his greatest sensory organ. His sense of smell is so great he can follow a trail that's weeks old, detect odors diluted to one-millionth the con-centration we'd need to notice them, even sniff out a person under water!

Taste: Dogs have fewer taste buds than we do, so they're likelier to try anything—and usually do, which is why it's especially impor-tant for their owners to monitor their food intake. Dogs are omni-vores, which means they eat meat as well as vegetable matter like grasses and weeds.

Touch: Dogs are social animals and love to be petted, groomed and played with.

Guardian Angels

Miniature Pinschers are vocal. This makes them excellent watch dogs. Usually, our dogs alert us long before the doorbell sounds, or when a car or person is on our property. Unfortunately, this trait makes them unsuitable for some apartment situations. They can be trained to be quiet, but not easily. And, if you train him in such a way, you will no longer have a guard dog. So it's a Catch-22. When I answer the door and the dogs are barking, I merely apologize and explain to my visitor that they are doing their job.

The barking characteristic can present a social problem. Guests can stimulate a Min Pin, and they tend to bark more than usual when people other than family are around. Some Min Pins are wary of strangers and can be reserved with new people. After a time, they normally accept visitors and warm up to them. If you are having a large group over to your house, it may be easier to confine your Min Pin until everyone has arrived and the activity level slows down.

The Min Pin in Your Home
The Min Pin and Children

Prospective owners often ask if the breed is good with children. Generally, the answer is yes. My conviction is that each dog is an individual, and just as siblings in a human family differ in personality, so do dogs in a breed and even in the same litter. Diva, a female I owned, adored children. She would literally shake with excitement when she saw a child! Some Min Pins prefer adults, and others are indifferent to people's ages. The child's behavior also influences the relationship.

Though each dog varies in its preference of the ages of its family members, if it is dealt with fairly and sensibly, almost any dog can be taught to accept people of all ages. Min Pins should not, however, be owned by families with very young children. Toddlers, like Min Pins, are very active. A baby who is learning to walk can be easily tripped by an exuberant dog. In addition, children aren't always gentle, and even a sturdy little dog can be injured if a baby playfully hits him with a hard object. If the dog's presence preceded that of the infant, you should teach the child to respect a pet just as he would a sibling. Likewise, the dog must be taught that the baby is a member of the family who must be treated gently.

THE MIN PIN AND OTHER PETS

When you have more than one dog, or if you have a playful cat, the Min Pin will often enjoy this companion. They sometimes tease each other with toys or food and growl protectively if another animal comes near their things. One of ours, Sultan, will not eat his meal until all the others are finished and then will hover over his food and take his time eating just to be a tease.

If you have multiple pets, it's important that you treat them equally, particularly when it comes to food. Be sure that when one gets a biscuit, they each get a biscuit. We call our dogs by name before we give them their treats (or else, they'd all jump for it!).

Most Miniature Pinschers get along well with other small dogs, but because they are totally unaware of their own size, they may challenge a much larger dog. My dogs consistently do. If you already have a medium-size or large pet, it must be a very gentle one, or else adding a Min Pin to the household is not advisable. Again, individual dogs respond differently to each other, and evaluating the possible chemistry between them is not always easy, even for a professional.

THE MIN PIN WEATHER REPORT

Min Pins love the outdoors in favorable weather, and some we've owned haven't always come in when called. Teaching them the word "come," praising them and providing a treat when they come in promptly, usually solves the problem. (I stress the word *usually*.) There are times when they can be naughty in a teasing way.

With our dogs, saying "time to eat!" works magic; and if it isn't mealtime, they are given a biscuit as a reward.

A sweater or a coat is needed for walks in the winter, though they don't seem to mind the snow at all and will have a good time romping in it while the snow is fresh. Once the snow hardens or turns icy, outdoor visits tend to become brief.

Min Pin Personality

CURIOUS CREATURES

Min Pins are inquisitive by nature. Anything new will catch their eye. Packages, particularly ones that contain food, intrigue them. Be aware not to leave grocery

bags or other foods within reach of a Min Pin. Foil or foam containers, boxes or bags are also doggie bait. If there's a chair near a counter or tabletop, you can be sure that a Min Pin will find a way to get to the "treat." Likewise, anything with your scent on it will have great appeal. Slippers and shoes, especially around teething puppies, are best left behind closed closet doors.

THE "CHILD" IN YOUR DOG

It has been said that having a dog as a pet is like having a perpetual three year old in the family.

Miniature Pinschers love to be outside in good weather— so much so that at times it's a chore to get them back inside!

Understanding and accepting this will greatly enhance your relationship with your dog. Once, when a client asked a friend's veterinarian how to raise her dog, the response was, "You raise your dog the same way you raise your children." A dog needs guidance, instruction and patience and for you to see his point of view. Most of all, a dog needs to be loved. The principles espoused by the famous Dr. Spock for your child can be applied to raising your canine as well.

Just like children, Min Pins will test you to see how much they can get away with. It's important that they understand who's the boss, and it's also important that they have a firm but kind master or mistress.

KEEPING TABS ON YOUR DOG

A Min Pin moves as fast as lightning. If he gets away, you can't outrun him. For this reason it's very important that he be walked with a well-fitted collar or harness. If he gets free, his curiosity will take over and

Miniature Pinschers are escape artists, so be sure that their area is secured.

you'll be faced with the problem of enticing him back. It's a rare Min Pin that you can trust off-lead. Everyone in the household, particularly children, must be very aware that the dog must be secured before a door is opened.

Because Min Pins have a tendency to flee, it is also vitally important that the backyard or play area be securely fenced in by a fence that is high enough so that your dog is unable to climb over it.

CHEW TOYS

This is a breed that likes to chew. They are excellent paper shredders. Tissues, bags and even newspapers can be targeted for ripping. Some are even hard on toys. Plush or fleece toys hold up best, but eventually even they may be pulled apart. *Larger* fleece or plush toys seem more durable than smaller ones. Because most dogs will remove and swallow any external parts in plush toys (such as plastic eyes), these kinds of toys should be avoided.

Hard vinyl toys get chewed to pieces quite quickly. Soft vinyl lasts a bit longer, but these will quickly lose their tiny noise makers. Handle all toys before giving them to your dog in order to leave your scent on them. Dogs seem to enjoy them more because of it. Be very careful with rawhide, unless you are able to watch while your dog chews it. Softened hide can easily choke a small dog. If you are going to feed your dog rawhide, give him larger pieces—and only when he can be supervised.

Getting Active

Can you find the Min Pin in this picture? These dogs love to burrow under the covers!

Because Min Pins are small and active, most can provide adequate exercise for themselves, even indoors. They will run quickly from room to room. The door bell or an unusual noise triggers action, too. On the other hand, they do not usually react to the phone, and they adjust easily to normal household sounds without responding.

WALKING THE DOG

Like any dog, Min Pins should be walked or permitted to exercise outdoors. However, they don't necessitate the mile-long walks required by larger breeds. Some Min Pins tend to be overactive and seemingly in perpetual motion. One of ours circles a great deal for no apparent reason whenever he anticipates going out or some activity.

Treat Your Dog with the Love He Deserves!

Every dog is very much an individual. Variations in behavior occur in part due to breeding, but most dogs are more the products of their environment than of their bloodlines. Even a breed as obviously proud and rugged as a Min Pin can be made to cower over time if given sufficient cause. As loving as this breed is, if treated harshly, your dog will respond with poor temperament. Each dog is a unique living being and if nurtured properly and kindly, he will give back in abundance the loyalty and friendship for which dogs have been known through the ages.

Frequently people ask if males or females are more affectionate. Again, I go back to my theory that dogs are individuals. I find both sexes equally loving with differences among various dogs. Yes, some dogs are naturally more affectionate than others, but it's not based on gender. Being an affectionate owner is the best way to ensure that you'll have an affectionate pet.

How to Talk to Your Dog

Most Min Pins are quite sensitive. Do not to use a harsh voice with them or scold them unnecessarily. Talking to your dog in a pleasant tone is extremely important. Use the dog's name often. Acknowledge the dog when you come home. Speak to your dog when he looks at you. Your voice is the most important sound in your pet's world, it is a vital element in bonding with your dog. You can make his day with just a few kind words, and it takes nothing more than to think about doing it.

CHARACTERISTICS OF THE MINATURE PINSCHER
Active
Curious
Intelligent
Loves to Eat
Sensitive to Odors
Persistent

Pet Your Dog

Dogs also respond positively to touch. Petting or stroking your Min Pin will soothe and calm him. They enjoy tremendously being massaged. Because they are so tiny, it takes only a minute or two to completely go over their bodies; and if you do, you'll have a happier and healthier pet. It's therapeutic for the owner as well. Recent studies have shown that petting a dog or cat lowers your blood pressure and improves your physical and mental health.

Most Min Pins can be lap dogs. They relish being cuddled, and love to be near you. When you sit down to read or write, they will anticipate some time on your lap. They know enough not to disturb meal times, but when dessert and coffee is served, they'll scramble for a cuddle. Likewise they will like to follow you around. Even when you shower, your dog may wait patiently on the bath mat for you to finish.

A Long-term Commitment

Miniature Pinschers live a long time. Small dogs generally have longer life spans than larger breeds. Min Pins also age more slowly and are puppy-like throughout their lives. After the age of fifteen they may become more sedate, but this is not always the case. Like humans, they vary in the age at which they start to gray. Often, the graying mask, and eventually the gray coat on the body, may be the only indication of their years. The lighter shading on their faces can be very attractive and striking especially with the black and rust colors. Teenage Min Pins are common, and some will live to be seventeen or eighteen years old. Keep this in mind when you choose to bring a puppy into your life—you are making a long-term commitment.

Traveling with Your Dog

Min Pins love to travel, but they are extremely territorial. Though this makes them excellent protectors, it also means that they will get fresh with anyone they perceive to be a possible threat to your property or your safety. For this reason, some will react at gas stations and toll booths with great assertiveness. However, as soon as you take them out of the car, they will have an immediate change of attitude and revert to being their normal friendly selves.

USE A CRATE!

It's best to crate a Min Pin for traveling. The swiftness of the breed presents the risk that they will dart when a door is opened. Their energy level means that they may move around in the car and interfere with your driving. Your dog may see it as lap time when you're behind the wheel. Should you need to stop short, that small body can be injured much more easily than a medium or large pet.

Several years ago, my husband's car was hit by a tractor-trailer and totaled on the New Jersey Turnpike. Three dogs were in separate crates in the back seat en route to our veterinarian for routine care. They were jarred but unharmed. Had they been free in the car, they would probably have been seriously, if not fatally, injured. For your own safety and that of your pet, crate your dogs when you travel. They will bark when you stop, but most often they will contentedly sleep during the trip and be ready for action when you arrive at your destination.

A Place to Play

Some owners without fenced-in yards use an exercise pen to give their Min Pin some outdoor time and to allow their pet to be with the family for a picnic or outing, albeit confined.

When they are outside, provide your dogs with a safe place to play.

Exercise pens, similar to children's playpens, are used extensively at dog shows. Once your pet gets used to one, the pen provides you with an alternative to walking your dog. It's a great advantage on days when you're running late, even though your Min Pin will miss his walk. If you use an exercise pen, a pen with vertical bars works best. (Those with horizontal bars can serve as ladders for these escape-artist dogs.)

At times, I find something (a piece of artwork, a story or a poem, for example) which fits the breed's profile so exactly that it needs to be shared. The poem "His Day," appeared as the last page in a book by Buris R. Boshell, M.D., titled *Your Miniature Pinscher.* Drummer Boy was owned by Dr. and Mrs. Boshell and had an outstanding record shown as a Champion. Special gratitude is extended to Martha Boshell for permission to reprint the poem here.

His Day

An Ode to Ch. Bo-Mar's Drummer Boy

He walked into the ring today,
His satin coat aglow.
He faced the Judge and seemed to say,
"I am here to win, you know."

"Behold my beauty unsurpassed,
A princely guy, I am.
I'm royally bred throughout my past,
Find better if you can."

An egotist this boy of mine?
I'm sure the Judge agreed.
But when he searched his heart and mind,
He gave him Best-of-Breed.

He won the Group, with flash and fire
And never missed his stride.
He strutted like a country squire
Beside himself with pride.

Now here he comes, his head held high
Stepping light and proud.
True and black, his eager eyes
Survey the waiting crowd.

He plants his feet and firmly stands.
Somehow, he seems to know,
The Trophy in the Judge's hands,
Proclaims him BEST-IN-SHOW.

—Barbara Andrews

To Learn More About the Miniature Pinscher

NATIONAL BREED CLUB

Miniature Pinscher Club of America, Inc.
Ms. Mary Selfies, Secretary
7600 E. Rio Verde Dr.
Tucson, AZ 85715

The club can give you information on all aspects of the breed, including the name and address of clubs and breeders in your area. There is also a national coordinator for Rescue.

NATIONAL BREED CLUB WEB SITE

http://members.aol.com/MPCA PEC

BOOKS

Boshell, Buris, R., MD. *Your Miniature Pinscher.* Denlinger's, 1969. (This book is currently out of print, but an updated version is in the course of being published by Martha Boshell.)

Coile, D. Caroline. *Miniature Pinscher—Everything about Purchase, Care, Nutrition, Breeding, Behavior and Training.* Hauppauge, NY: Barron's Educational Series, 1996.

O'Neil, Jacqueline. *A New Owner's Guide to Miniature Pinschers.* Neptune City, NJ: T.F.H. Publications, 1997.

Tietjen, Sari Brewster. *The New Miniature Pinscher.* New York: Howell Book House, 1988.

MAGAZINE

Pinscher Patter
Jane C. Garvin, Editor
1922 SW Mawcrest Court
Gresham, OR 07080-5722

Printed quarterly, this is the official publication of the Miniature Pinscher Club of America, Inc.

VIDEO

Miniature Pinschers
American Kennel Club
55580 Centerview Drive
Raleigh, NC 27606-3390
(919) 233-9767

Living
with a

Miniature Pinscher

Bringing Your
Miniature
Pinscher
Home

The Delta Society in Renton, Washington, is an organization dedicated to the interactions among people, animals and the environment. It's president, Leo K. Bustad, D.V.M., Ph.D., states, "Our survival as a species depends on our ability to foster a boundless compassion for living things. A person or community is not healthy without nurturing contact with animals and nature."

Pets are unique friends whom you can talk to and who will never be judgmental. They are wonderful for your ego—always overjoyed to see you. They are sure to force you to go out and get your exercise, even when you normally might feel too tired to do so. And, they are marvelous companions especially for those who live alone.

In order to enjoy your new pet to the fullest, you must be a responsible dog owner. Dogs are a commitment in time, care and expense. You will need to make changes not only in your home but in your daily schedule in order to provide for your new Miniature Pinscher's needs.

Making the Right Choice

Selecting the right animal to share your life with should not be rushed. Do your homework in advance. You have taken the correct first step by reading about the breed you are considering. If possible, go to a dog show or two and speak with breeders. Ask many questions and learn all you can about your preliminary breed choice.

Once you've decided on a Miniature Pinscher, visit as many breeders as your schedule permits. Responsible breeders will not only answer all your questions, they will question you about previous dogs you and your family might have owned and how you plan to care for your new pup. That concern should give you confidence that this is a reliable breeder who cares what type of home the puppy will have.

Finding Your Puppy

BREEDERS

Finding a good breeder is a necessary chore when adopting your dog. A good breeder will give you detailed instructions for the care and feeding of your pet. She will also give you your dog's health history and will encourage you to call her if you have any questions before and after you choose one of her dogs.

A good breeder will also expect you to have your Min Pin checked by your veterinarian to satisfy everyone that the dog is sound and in good health. Finally, she'll give you registration papers and a three-generation pedigree. A "limited registration" may be used for animals that are not intended for breeding.

SELECTING YOUR PUP

When selecting your puppy, pay close attention to
how she responds to you. A decision to own a particular dog should not be impulsive. The best age to bring
home a puppy is at twelve weeks. Some breeders, however prefer to sell their
puppies at a later age
so that they can deter-
mine which puppies
in the litter have the
greatest show potential.

Many breeders prefer
to have their puppies
go to a new home with
their ears cropped.
Post-surgical care for
this procedure can be
challenging for the novice. As previously stated, the
ears do not have to be cropped, and a breeder may permit you to take home a puppy at a younger age if the
ears are to be left natural. Cropping is usually done
when a puppy is at least several weeks old (it can be
done anytime thereafter as well).

*A reputable
breeder will help
you choose the
right puppy for
you.*

BREED RESCUE

Many shelters will contact kennel clubs' rescue com-
mittees. "Breed rescue" is designed to place animals
whose owners were not capable of caring for them into
a good home. These dogs are emerging from a wide
range of circumstances. Some of them might be older.
If the dog was found on the street, her background
might be unknown. Some dogs come to the club
handed over directly from their owners.

Some clubs, such as the Miniature Pinscher Club, will
place a rescued dog in a foster home (usually the home
of one of its members). Here, the dog's health, both
physical and emotional, are evaluated. Veterinary care
and spay or neuter surgery are also provided. In the
meantime, the rescue committee will try to place the
dog with an owner that is most compatible with her.

If you decide to adopt from a rescue organization, you will need to fill out an application, agree to return the dog if you decide not to keep her and give the club a small donation to help cover the costs of care. You will be given whatever information the club has on the Min Pin. Keep in mind that a dog who has bonded with someone else in her "past life" can transfer that bond to you—so don't be overly concerned if you are not taking a puppy.

Homeward Bound

Acquiring a new pet is always an exciting time for the entire family. Whether it's a warm and cuddly little puppy or an adult, that Min Pin is, like you, experiencing a dramatic change in her life. If she is a puppy, she is being taken away from her littermates and her mother. All dogs are leaving familiar surroundings for a totally strange place and new people. You can help make this transition easier and a lot less stressful by some advance preparation. There are a number of basic things you will need for your dog.

FOOD AND WATER BOWLS

A food and water bowl are absolutely necessary. Stainless steel ones, preferably weighted to keep them from tipping, are best. Ceramic is fine as well. Plastic can and will be chewed, and it is also prone to have crevices in it where bacteria can linger.

FOOD

Dog food is an obvious necessity. Your breeder should advise you which food the puppy has been eating, and she will probably also give you a small amount to get you started. Because a puppy is fed three times a day, it's best to buy a good deal of food.

A LEASH AND COLLAR

Two other necessities are a leash and a collar. Remember, you are bringing home a small puppy, so don't purchase a heavy leash or collar expecting to use

**PUPPY
ESSENTIALS**

Your new
puppy will
need:

food bowl

water bowl

collar

leash

ID tag

bed

crate

toys

grooming
supplies

it when the puppy grows up. For a young pup, a light collar and leash usually work best.

A narrow collar will not rub the coat as much as a wide one. It's a good idea to place a tag with your name, your dog's name and your phone number on the collar or harness as well.

A PLACE TO SLEEP

Your dog will need a bed or some other suitable place to sleep. There are many quality beds on the market. Even a sturdy box is fine. The bed should be lined with soft towels or washable blankets. It should be set in a draft-free location.

Your dog will need a place to sleep. Any of the quality beds available are suitable.

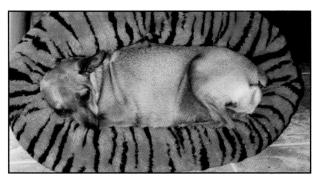

PLAYTHINGS

Your puppy needs to play, and a large plush or fleece toy will keep her amused and occupied for hours on end. The toys you select must be safe. Since the puppy may be teething, she might chew right through toys that have squeakers on the surface. These squeakers can be swallowed and cause your dog to choke. Several chew toys are a must. Puppies like to chew, and safe chew toys will keep your new pet away from your things.

Note that toys that are made of string are not safe for a teething pup. Puppies have been known to tear them apart and ingest the string which can become entwined in the intestines.

Puppy-Proofing Your Home

After you've got all your tools in order, the next step is to puppy-proof your home. Look around every room in which your puppy will be allowed, and remove anything that can be a potential danger. Puppy-proofing your house is very much like baby-proofing your house. Minimize the opportunity for injury by applying forethought and common sense. A puppy doesn't perceive danger any more than a child does.

TURNING DANGEROUS AREAS INTO SAFE AREAS

Most kitchens, bathrooms and garages present a danger, as they house many toxic substances. Potentially harmful chemicals such as cleaning compounds, gardening supplies and pesticides should all be stored securely, well out of your dog's reach, in a closed and preferably locked cabinet or closet. Because it is harder to puppy-proof a garage (some of the chemicals may have spilled on the floor), it is usually best not to let your dog roam around in there at all.

Wires and Cords

Tuck away dangling electric wires and cords. Put them out of the dog's reach so that she can't chew them. They are a hazard not only because they can cause her to electrocute herself, but also because she can get caught in the wires. Venetian blind cords are also dangerous, and a puppy can strangle herself if she gets entangled in them.

Poisonous Plants

Some plants are poisonous, too. Harmful plants can be found both inside the house and out. The American Kennel Club Health Foundation publishes a list of plants that are

---

HOUSEHOLD DANGERS

Curious puppies and inquisitive dogs get into trouble not because they are bad, but simply because they want to investigate the world around them. It's our job to protect our dogs from harmful substances, like the following:

IN THE HOUSE

cleaners, especially pine oil

perfumes, colognes, aftershaves

medications, vitamins

office and craft supplies

electric cords

chicken or turkey bones

chocolate

some house and garden plants, like ivy, oleander and poinsettia

IN THE GARAGE

antifreeze

garden supplies, such as snail and slug bait, pesticides, fertilizers, mouse and rat poisons harmful to dogs. This list can, and should, be requested from the American Kennel Club.

RESTRICTED ACCESS

It's advisable to section off an area in your home where your dog can be safely confined until she feels comfortable and secure in your home. Preventing your dog from having free reign over your home also helps during housetraining and prevents your puppy from getting underfoot or hurt in some other way. In addition, a puppy needs a fair amount of rest, and having her own private retreat is beneficial for all involved.

CHECKUP TIME

Preferably, your first visit to your veterinarian should be scheduled before you bring your dog home so that you can visit her straight off, while en route from the breeder's kennel to your home. The veterinarian will

perform a full checkup in order to detect if there are any health concerns. (If there are any potential serious health problems, return the puppy from where you bought her immediately.)

The health record provided by the breeder will determine when future vaccinations are due.

A stuffed toy can become the perfect plaything for your dog.

Your veterinarian should be consulted on any questions you may have and advise you on the medical care that your pet requires. Never hesitate to call your veterinarian or the breeder when questions arise.

The Big Day
FIRST THINGS FIRST

Familiar odors help the puppy to adapt to its new residence. When the day comes and you are ready to bring the newcomer home, bring a towel or blanket with you. Ask the breeder to rub the fabric on the mother or ask the person who has been caring for the puppy to handle it. Doing either of these things will leave a familiar scent on the cloth. The cloth or towel will then act as a security blanket while the puppy adjusts to your home. Your Min Pin will be nervous from all the excitement and may get car sick or have an accident. Wrapping her in another towel while driving home is advisable.

CARRYING YOUR MIN PIN

When you carry the puppy, be sure to support her back. If necessary, use two hands to lift her. Min Pins of any age should be carried on the arm and supported by your hand. Your fingers should keep the two front legs together. It is also helpful not to spread her legs during the growing weeks—the shoulders will only develop in place if the front legs are not constantly spread apart. An adult dog will probably rest on your arm with its rear on your hip for support.

ARRIVING HOME

If you already have a pet, it's best to put him outdoors or in another room until your new dog or puppy is brought in. Then, let the puppy investigate her surroundings. Show the dog her quarters and her bed. Let her know where the water bowl is located and allow her to sniff around. Even though the puppy won't understand you yet, talk to her in soft tones as if she does. This will help your Min Pin to get used to your voice and feel more secure. Decide on a name for your puppy immediately and use it as often as possible. Two-syllable names work best for when you want to train later on.

INTRODUCING YOUR OTHER PETS

After your Min Pin has become well acquainted with her new surroundings, bring in your cat or first dog and again talk to them in a reassuring way. Be sure to supervise the meeting. If you are not able to watch them closely, keep them separated.

Depending on the size of your older pet, you may need to confine the puppy until she is fully grown and becomes friends with the pet you already have. Above all, be sure that the older pet doesn't get jealous. Give extra attention to your first cat or dog for a while so that the new addition isn't viewed as a threat. Use the same principles as you would with older siblings if you were bringing a new baby home.

Children and Your Dog

Young children must be taught that your Miniature Pinscher is a living creature—not a toy. Children should understand that the dog must be treated gently, and they should be taught to behave calmly around her. Sudden movements and running around early on may startle the pet and cause her to grab at a hand or leg with her mouth because she feels threatened. Even when petting the newcomer, children should be gentle. Once they start to play with the Min Pin, be certain that they don't overdo it—a puppy, like a baby, tires easily.

Once everyone has been introduced, the puppy needs to rest. It's best not to have visitors for the first day or two until the puppy settles in. It is also best to avoid bringing a new puppy or dog during the holidays. The additional activity is added stress to the new arrival. In addition, the family is distracted with the celebrations and visitors and is often too busy to give the puppy the time and attention that she requires.

Provide Your Pet with Company

If at all possible, have someone at home for the first few days after the puppy or new dog arrives. Dogs experience separation anxiety. They feel uncomfortable when left alone, especially at first. If it is not possible for someone to be home, leave a radio playing soft music or a tape of someone speaking. Keep the volume low. Dogs have sensitive hearing. It helps to leave the puppy with its favorite toy and a scented item of your clothing that you no longer plan to wear. Also, always leave on a happy note talking to your pet. I usually say in a pleasant voice, "Mind the house." With your help, your dog will outgrow separation anxiety.

Your puppy may cry for the first few nights that she is in your home, so scheduling a weekend for the homecoming is often best. Providing the puppy with a hot-water bottle and a ticking clock, both of which should be wrapped in a soft cloth or towel, will simulate the mother's warmth and heartbeat. Don't yell at the puppy for fussing. As a rule, a gentle, reassuring voice will accomplish more. But at the same time, don't go to the puppy every time she whimpers, as that will only encourage her to continue to whine.

Remember: Your pup has just been separated from her mom. You will need to work hard to make her feel at home.

KEEP YOUR DOG AT HOME UNTIL FULLY IMMUNIZED

It's not only important to try to avoid having visitors right after the puppy arrives home, but it's also not a good idea take your Min Pin out. The exposure to germs prior to the puppy having all of her permanent vaccinations is extremely risky. Wait until the puppy has had all of her inoculations and your veterinarian tells you that it's absolutely safe before taking her visiting.

BE A GOOD DOGGIE NEIGHBOR

Being a good dog neighbor is vitally important, and you should take the necessary steps in order to be one. Don't allow your dog to soil your neighbors' lawn, scare their youngsters, tease their cat or dog or dig up their garden. Keep the dog on your property even when she's on lead. Obey your community's laws on licensing. Clean up after your dog. Curb your Min Pin when you walk her, even if it is not required by municipal regulations. Dogs learn quickly, and so it's up to you to set the guidelines.

Never allow your Min Pin to roam. Not only is it dangerous but it can be annoying to others. Be sure that your dog has some ID. This can be done in many different ways. The traditional way is to use a tag. Alternatively, you can have your dog tattooed, or your veterinarian can insert a microchip into the shoulder/back area. Many shelters, police departments and, of course, veterinarians now have scanners to read microchips, so a lost pet that has had a microchip implanted can be returned to her owner.

Clean Up After Your Dog

Keep your own property clean, too. Train your pet to confine her toilet needs to one area. Carry the dog to that spot after meals, the first thing in the morning or for its final evening outing. Urine burns grass and by doing this you will prevent your dog from ruining your lawn. You will also only need to pooper scoop in one area. It takes a little extra effort to formulate good habits but in the long run, it is well worth it.

There are scooping gadgets available in all pet stores that make it easy to clean up without having to bend down. For your own convenience, the early morning and late evening outings can be shorter—it can just be a time for the dog to relieve herself. Longer walks are better when time permits.

Avoid Annoying the Neighbors

Bring your dog into the house if she is barking, whining or howling. This type of behavior can grate on your neighbors' nerves. There's a simple test for being a responsible neighbor. Ask yourself, "Would I want my neighbor's pet to behave as mine does?"

SOCIALIZATION

Once you have your veterinarian's approval to take the dog on outings, the need to socialize your Min Pin starts. I highly recommend Kindergarten Puppy

Training or KPT. This training is structured specifically for puppies and is used to teach basic commands and to acquaint your puppy with people and other dogs. The instructor will show you how to strengthen the bond between yourself and the Min Pin. He under-

stands that puppies have short attention spans and will suggest that you limit your training sessions at home to ten minutes at a time. You and the dog will learn a lot. When the puppy is older, novice or basic obedience classes are a *must*.

Once your dog has started her socializa-

Socializing your puppy is one of the most important aspects of being a Min Pin owner.

tion process, introduce your pet to service people, particularly if your dog is fenced in, while they deliver your mail, newspaper and so on. Tell them your dog's name so that they can get acquainted. Give them treats to give your Min Pin. It encourages a good relationship.

When you do let your Min Pin out to play, it is best not to tie the dog to a tree or other object. This encourages aggression—probably more so in a breed with natural guarding instincts than one without.

Never leave a dog unattended with an infant in the room—both have the potential to be hurt. Do not use a crate just for travel; use one also for the times when you have service people inside, have an infant crawling on the floor or are cleaning and don't want the Min Pin under-foot. A dog that is crate broken has a safe place to rest when it's too dangerous for her to be around. Many will sleep in their crates or use it as a place of refuge. I feed my dogs in crates so I know which has eaten. During the day, the crate doors are open, and my Min Pins rest in them when they want to get away from the action.

47

TRAINING TIPS

All dogs need to be trained, and training will be discussed in depth in chapter 8. The following tips will help get you started as you socialize your pup.

When Not to Call Your Dog

Never call a Min Pin to you to in order to administer corrective discipline. The next time you call, she'll remember and head in the opposite direction. Any sensible dog will not come to you readily when you summon her again after you've called her only to discipline her.

It's best never to call a dog to you for something unpleasant. If you're going to trim nails or administer medication she doesn't like, go to the dog and pick her up—*do not call her to come to you.*

Consistency and Praise

The twin secrets of success in training this breed are consistency and praise. Ending a training session on a positive note is a definite plus and will help set the stage for the next lesson. Be positive—if you enjoy training, your dog will enjoy it, too!

If you want to earn your dog's confidence, be sure that she understands the command in training before you start a correction. Be persistent in your repetition of positive reinforcement until you are totally certain your Min Pin knows what you're asking her to do. Only when you're sure that she is deliberately *not* obeying should you correct her.

Some Final Words on Training

Of course, timing is crucial and any correction must be immediate, or your Min Pin will not know why she's being corrected. Also *correct,* don't *punish,* if you want to be successful. Because of their small size, teaching Min Pins the "sit," "down," "stand" and "stay" commands is easier on a table, washing machine, cabinet or other elevated platform. If you cover the surface with a towel, not only will your dog not slide, she'll be more comfortable. It's a lot easier than bending down. Another alternative is to sit on a stair and have your Min Pin a step above you or on the landing while you work. This brings you to the dog's level, too, and enhances learning. And remember—if you're having fun, chances are your Min Pin will, too.

If you are unable to get to classes, then read some training books. Any time spent on training your dog will pay high dividends throughout her life, and it will make the dog much more of a joy to have around.

chapter 5

Feeding
Your
Miniature
Pinscher

New pet foods appear on the market constantly. Pet food is available in three varieties: canned, dry and semi-moist. Most are formulated for specific ages: "Puppy" or "Growth" formula is fed to a growing dog, "Adult" or "Maintenance" to a mature dog and "Senior" to an aging dog. "Lite" or "Reducing" formulas help to keep an overweight pet trim. A huge assortment of menu choices and foods is also available to meet activity levels from stress to maintenance to inactive. Veterinary hospitals carry prescription diet products, which are foods formulated for specific health needs, providing proper nutrients for dogs with kidney and heart problems. They are formulated to modify the level of certain nutrients that may aggravate the specific health condition.

Start with Familiar Food

With all the choices, how do you know which food is best for your Min Pin?

Start by feeding a new puppy or adult the food that your Min Pin was being fed before you brought him home. Keeping the same feeding schedule is also advisable. Changes in diet almost always cause diarrhea. With the stress of relocation, adding intestinal upset to your Miniature Pinscher's life should be avoided. Diet changes should be postponed until your pet is well established in your home. Then, any change in food must occur slowly. Begin by adding very small quantities of the new food to what is presently being fed, and gradually increase the amount.

A Balanced Diet

Proper diet is as important to dogs as it is to humans. Because the Min Pin is small and requires relatively limited quantities of food, top quality is essential. Feed your dog the best food you can find and afford.

NUTRITIONAL REQUIREMENTS

Learn to read dog food labels. As you may know from your own foods, ingredients are listed in descending order based on content. Labels should always show a "Statement of Nutritional Adequacy." The label must state how the diet meets the standards set by the American Association of Feed Control Officials' nutrient profiles

---

HOW TO READ THE DOG FOOD LABEL

With so many choices on the market, how can you be sure you're feeding the right food for your dog? The information's all there on the label—if you know what you're looking for.

Look for the nutritional claim right up top. Is the food "100% nutritionally complete?" If so, it's for nearly all life stages; "growth and maintenance," on the other hand, is for early development; puppy foods are marked as such, as are senior foods.

Ingredients are listed in descending order by weight. The first three or four ingredients will tell you the bulk of what the food contains. Look for the highest-quality ingredients, like meats and grains, to be among them.

The Guaranteed Analysis tells you what level of protein, fat, fiber and moisture are in the food, in that order. While these numbers are meaningful, they won't tell you much about the quality of the food. Nutritional value is in the dry matter, not the moisture content. In many ways, seeing is believing.

If your dog has bright eyes, shiny coat, a good appetite and a good energy level, chances are his diet's fine. Your dog's breeder and your veterinarian are good sources of advice if you're still confused.

for dogs. For instance, the label may show that the food is "complete and balanced" for a particular age such as puppy/growth or adult/maintenance or is suitable for any age.

Know that "beef by-products" are not the same as "beef." By-products are body parts which often cannot be included in foods meant for human consumption. There's usually no harm in feeding food with by-products, but an all-meat product is certainly preferable.

The basic food group requirements for dogs are similar to ours. An ideal meal includes proteins, fats and carbohydrates in the proper proportions. Vitamins and minerals play an important role as well. Research has established exactly how much dogs of various sizes need and the amounts are usually specified on the label. You may find that since Min Pins are so active and energetic, you need to feed more than the recommended amount in order to maintain correct weight on yours.

Developing a Feeding Schedule

The following chart explains the recommended feeding schedule based on a Min Pin's age:

Age	Frequency of Meals Daily
8 weeks to 3 months	4 to 5
3 to 6 months	3
6 months on, for life	2

A puppy will often tell you when it's time to eliminate a feeding by not finishing one of his meals. Small dogs do best on two meals throughout life. The two meals for an adult dog need not be identical. You can feed dry food only in the morning, and the evening meal can consist of dry food with some canned.

Because Min Pins are such good eaters, the "demand-feeding" or "free-feeding" that is ideal for some breeds normally doesn't work for Min Pins. Your dog will eat everything you give him and, if not placed on a schedule, he will surely overeat.

Feed your dog all of his meals in the same place and on the same schedule. Select a quiet area where the Miniature Pinscher will not be disturbed. Children should be taught that the dog is protective of his food and may snap if he feels that the food is going to be taken away while he's eating. For this reason, urge children to leave the Min Pin alone during meals.

Regardless of whether or not your dog has eaten, remove the food bowl after fifteen minutes. This will teach him that he is to eat when the food is served. Normally, Min Pins eat as soon as the food is put down. Occasionally, they may miss a meal, but if your dog doesn't eat two or three successive meals, view it as a sign for concern and call the veterinarian.

Water

Your dog should have clean, fresh water available at *all* times. Don't just refill the water bowl; empty it daily and wash it before refilling it. Water bowls collect a film of residue at the bottom that must be removed. Because Miniature Pinschers do not drink great quantities of water, you may consider giving your dog bottled water.

Water is one of the most important elements of your dog's diet.

Treats and Table Scraps

Your Miniature Pinscher will enjoy an occasional treat such as a dog biscuit. Keep the quantity limited by using the smallest-sized treats you can find. You might even want to break biscuits in half for puppies. If your Min Pin is very active and at an ideal body weight, it's

53

OK to give it extra treats. Keep an eye on its tuck-up or waistline—the area just beyond the rib cage. If it doesn't curve up, limit the treats. Always avoid anything spicy, salty or greasy, which may cause intestinal upset.

FOODS TO PROTECT YOUR DOG AGAINST

There are foods that we eat which are potentially deadly for dogs. Chocolate, which contains theobromine, is toxic to dogs and can cause serious and even fatal illness. Never leave candy on a table where it can be reached by your Miniature Pinscher. Even if it's sealed in a box, members of this breed can chew through to get to the tasty-smelling chocolate.

The proper diet will ensure that your dog stays in shape.

Onions are also very dangerous and tend to impair the dog's blood chemistry causing severe anemia and even death. This applies to all colors and variations of onions and chives. Garlic should also be avoided even if the small amounts used for seasoning aren't likely to reach toxic levels. It's better to be safe than sorry.

It doesn't take much with a Min Pin's small body to cause devastating problems. Remember, not everything that tastes good to your dog is good for him. The responsibility for feeding a dog properly rests totally with the owner.

TIME FOR A DIET

Dogs gain weight for the same reasons people do. Overfeeding a Min Pin is ever-so-tempting. When the caloric intake of your dog exceeds the energy that he uses, the body stores whatever is left over as fat. The heavier a dog becomes, the less likely he is to exercise, and so he gains even more weight.

Min pins differ from one another in how they burn calories. Heredity influences thyroid function, and some dogs are more prone to obesity than others. This breed doesn't have long hair to hide its weight, so you will readily notice when your Min Pin is gaining weight.

Feeding your Min Pin a little less of its regular food daily by gradually reducing the portion is another approach to helping it reach ideal weight. Adding some vegetables such as string beans to his food will satisfy his hunger without adding many calories.

Above all, don't feed an overweight dog high-calorie treats. If a dieting Min Pin begs for food, take him for a nice walk or play with him instead. You'll be showing your Min Pin a great kindness.

> ### TO SUPPLEMENT OR NOT TO SUPPLEMENT?
>
> If you're feeding your dog a diet that's correct for his developmental stage and he's alert, healthy looking and neither overweight nor underweight, you don't need to provide supplements. These include table scraps as well as vitamins and minerals. In fact, a growing puppy is in danger of developing musculoskeletal disorders through oversupplementation. If you have any concerns about the nutritional quality of the food you're feeding, discuss them with your veterinarian.

The Older Dog

Aging dogs tend to gain weight primarily because of reduced activity. Accommodate this change in lifestyle by feeding one of the senior diets or by reducing his caloric intake. Older dogs may also suddenly start losing weight. One of our geriatric males started losing weight slowly for no obvious reason. Our veterinarian attributed it to the fact that an older dog's system may no longer process the food as efficiently as it once did, resulting in weight loss. Increasing his food intake and providing additional supplements has stabilized his weight.

Assessing Your Dog's Eating Habits

The best way to know if your Min Pin is eating right is to take an analytical look at him at least once a week. Is he the correct weight? Does his coat shine? Are his eyes bright and alert? What is his energy level and general disposition?

A dog's feces is the best way to tell if he has an intestinal problem. A good diet produces a well-formed firm stool, and the bowels are regularly eliminated. Constipation and diarrhea can have many causes, one of which is dietary change or even the treats he's eating. Abnormal color, such as a green tint to the stool can be an indication of food dyes or additives. These additives are no better for your dog than they are for you. Some additives are used to add eye appeal to the food in order to tempt you to purchase it, but they do nothing favorable for your pet. Soft-moist foods are convenient to feed but contain high amounts of preservatives, sugar, salt and often dye

chapter 6

Grooming
Your
Miniature
Pinscher

Imagine how nice it would be if you never had to set or comb your hair or have it cut or styled and yet it still always looked perfectly groomed. While we can never experience such luxury for ourselves, we can almost achieve it with our pet if she is a Miniature Pinscher. Brief, periodic brushing is all it takes to keep a Miniature Pinscher looking like the queen that she is. It's a breed tailor-made for today's busy lives.

A Min Pin's coat is her crowning glory. It gleams in the sun. There's never a time nor a season during the year when the coat looks unkempt as can happen with long-coated breeds.

Checking over Your Dog

As with any dog, the nails, teeth, ears and eyes of Min Pins need regular attention. Brushing is minimal and bathing infrequent. Even if a Min Pin gets wet or muddy, it merely calls for a quick once-over with a towel to clean and dry it.

You will find that it is always easier to groom a dog that has a working "vocabulary." In this respect, it is important to give your Min Pin some basic obedience training. A dog that knows what "sit," "stand," "stay" and "no" mean is far better equipped to cooperate when being groomed.

EYES

The eyes of a Min Pin don't tear very much, but some matter can collect in the corner—especially overnight. This is easily wiped away with a wet cotton ball. The eyes are apt to tear a bit during the allergy season when pollen counts are high. Should the hair below the eye become stained, clean it with a wet piece of cotton, dry it with a tissue and then apply a thin coat of Vaseline™

Ear care is extremely important to your dog's health.

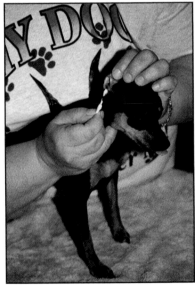

so that the tears just roll off. If the eye is red or inflamed, or if there is excessive prolonged tearing, consult your veterinarian. Except for the saline solution, don't medicate the eyes using anything else, unless prescribed by your veterinarian.

EARS

Unless your pet is scratching, shaking her head or her ear is emitting a foul odor, checking the Miniature Pinscher's ears every three or four weeks is adequate. Clean the outer folds and crevices carefully with an ear wash (available in pet stores), or use peroxide and a piece of cotton. Ear cleaning solutions are also available from your veterinarian. Follow the directions on the container. Usually, they call for using two or three drops of the cleaner and then rubbing the ear to loosen any dirt or wax. Your dog will probably shake her head to remove the excess. Wax deposits should be gently removed using a moistened cotton swab or piece of cotton. If you decide to use a cotton swab, be extremely careful never to go into the inner ear. Just clean the part of the ear that is visible to you.

A foul odor or any inflammation can mean your dog might have ear mites or an infection in the inner ear canal. A veterinarian should be contacted immediately, as this can be painful for the dog and hard to treat if left unattended for long.

TEETH

It's advantageous to get a puppy accustomed to having her mouth examined. Always be gentle and use a reassuring tone of voice. This will enable you to check

Regular dental care will ensure strong teeth.

her mouth, clean her teeth and administer pills whenever necessary. It will also make life easier when she is examined by your veterinarian.

Dogs, like people, grow two sets of teeth. The baby, or deciduous, teeth normally come in at

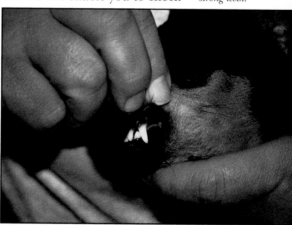

three to five weeks. The permanent teeth emerge at sixteen to thirty weeks of age. The gums can be tender when a puppy is teething and can also be swollen or inflamed, which in turn can affect the puppy's appetite. Dogs have a total of forty-two permanent teeth.

It's wise to begin to clean a Miniature Pinscher's teeth early on. Wrap some gauze around your finger and

59

moisten it with a few drops of water. Dip the gauze into a little baking soda and rub it over the teeth to clean them. *Do not use a toothpaste designed for humans.* There are many liquid preparations and toothpastes designed especially for dogs. A baby's tooth brush is fine to use, but you can also get one that is made for dogs.

Dogs, like people, have tartar build up. Dry food and biscuits help to control this problem. Using your thumb nail to scrape the tartar off the teeth works quite well. It is not recommended that dental instruments be used because they can scratch the tooth, and if a tooth is scratched, it can attract bacteria.

NAILS

Short nails are essential to healthy feet. Long nails are detrimental to the bone structure in the feet and cause the toes to spread out. Nails curve over when long and can become deformed. Longer nails are also harder to trim because of the curve. Curved nails can catch on a fence or piece of furniture and hurt the dog. For these reasons, it is essential to keep your dog's nails trimmed at all times. Trim the nails every two weeks to keep them short and blunt. If this is not possible, consider having a groomer or your veterinarian do them on a regularly scheduled basis.

Most dogs do not like to have their nails clipped. It's best to start manicuring the nails at an early age so that the puppy gets used to it. Gently touching and handling the feet of your dog while the puppy is still young can also ease resistance during subsequent nail trimmings.

You may be able to use clippers designed for human nails for this chore when the Min Pin is young. Later on, select either one of the manual dog clippers or an electric grinder. You will also need a file or an emery board to smooth the nails after clipping.

Dogs have a blood vessel or vein in each nail known as the "quick." Frequent nail trims will make the quick recede so you can keep the nails short without cutting the quick.

GROOMING TOOLS

pin brush

slicker brush

flea comb

towel

matt rake

grooming glove

scissors

nail clippers

tooth-cleaning equipment

shampoo

conditioner

clippers

Because Min Pins have dark nails, the quick cannot be seen as it can in dogs with light-colored nails. If you should cut the quick, it will bleed. Keep styptic powder or a blood-clotting product like alum available when you trim nails. An injured quick may make your dog resent having her nails cut.

Grooming the Coat

A meticulously groomed dog looks and feels great. Coat and skin condition starts with proper nutrition. Adequate exercise also contributes to a healthy coat. A dry coat and excessive shedding may be a sign of a poor diet, or even illness.

BRUSHING

Establish a routine for grooming your dog, and be consistent. Because the Miniature Pinscher requires so little grooming and always looks so good, some owners get lax about this responsibility. It's just as important to maintain a short coat as a long one, it's just a lot easier.

The coat should be brushed at least once a week. By placing the dog on a table or bench, you won't have to bend over and you'll be closer to your dog. A rubber mat or towel will secure your dog's footing. Using a table will also teach the dog to be comfortable when she is taken to the veterinarian's office and examined. Remember *never* to leave a Min Pin on a table unattended or she is likely to jump off.

Groom your dog from head to toe! Nail trimming is a crucial part of total care.

To comb out the coat, use a soft brush, a piece of folded velvet or other soft fabric, or a rubber mitt or glove. Brushes and grooming mitts are sold in pet

61

supply stores. If you're using fabrics, you can probably find them around your home.

Start at the head and work back, brushing with the grain of the hair. This will clean the coat, distribute the natural oils, stimulate the skin and remove dead hair. Check for fleas and ticks as you groom, especially in summer months. Parasites thrive in warm weather.

It's recommended that your pet receive a treat after a grooming session. (Our dogs always remember and look forward to the reward.)

BATHING YOUR DOG

Bathe your Min Pin only when she really needs it—this may be as infrequently as every six months. Do not bathe a puppy until she is several months old. (You can use baby wipes available in all supermarkets to clean off a young puppy.)

If possible, use a sink when bathing your Min Pin. This will be easier for you and give you more control over your dog. A bathtub is the second choice but will mean that you have to kneel while you give the bath.

You will need a number of items to bathe your pet. Make sure that you prepare these materials before you attempt to bathe your dog. You will need cotton balls, shampoo for dogs (you can find this in a pet supply store), a plastic cup, mineral oil, two or three towels, a sponge or face cloth, and whatever you are using to brush the coat. You may also want a waterproof apron for yourself because there will undoubtedly be water flying everywhere!

Consistent grooming is the way to keep your dog looking and feeling great!

Getting Started

Brush your dog first to remove any loose hairs. Place a cotton ball in each ear and a drop of mineral oil in each eye to protect your Min Pin from shampoo and water.

Fill the sink or tub with warm water no higher than the dog's elbows. When you lift your dog up to put her in the water, speak to her in a reassuring way. Tell her that you are going to give her a nice warm bath; it helps—especially for that first bath a puppy experiences.

Washing Your Dog

Using the cup, pour the warm water over the body, but not the head. Be careful not to get any water in the ears. Then, wet the sponge or face cloth and clean the dog's head. Apply the shampoo over the entire coat. Wash from the chin down, but avoid the face and especially the eyes. Rub in the shampoo, being certain to do the underside and the genitals. Rinse several times using the cup. Incomplete rinsing dulls the coat and may irritate the skin, causing the dog to scratch.

A great deal of time is spent grooming a dog before her grand entrance into the show ring, but the pet Min Pin is easy to maintain.

Use a clean wash cloth to remove the excess water. Then fully towel dry your dog. You may have to use at least two towels to absorb whatever water remains. Be sure to dry the outside and inside of the ears thoroughly. In the cooler months, don't allow your dog outdoors for at least an hour or until she is fully dry. Likewise, be sure to always dry your Miniature Pinscher after she goes out in the rain. A short coat can absorb an amazing amount of water.

After a bath, the skin sometimes appears to produce flakes or dandruff. This may be due to inadequate rinsing but not always. Pour a small amount of Listerine™ on a soft cloth and wipe down your dog to help eliminate the dandruff. It may also help to put a "leave in" conditioner on the coat and rub it in well. The creme vanishes into the coat and leaves it glowing.

63

Keeping Your
Miniature
Pinscher
Healthy

The first step in keeping your Miniature Pinscher healthy and safe, is to prevent accidents from happening. There are a number of things that you must take care of in order to insure that your dog will remain out of harm's way.

Accident-Proof Your Home

The following is a checklist to use in order to make sure your home is as safe as possible for your pet:

- Telephone, electrical, drapery and venetian blind cords can be just as dangerous for an adult dog as for a puppy. Keep them out of reach of your dog.

- Keep any window that your dog can get to, even from a chair or sofa, open from the top only.

- Secure your garbage. Foil, wrappings and containers with the smell of food should be kept in a tightly covered trash can. Min Pins will chew them and swallow anything that contains food remnants.

- Do not use poison of any kind, including ant traps, inside or around your home.

- Keep all medications—the dog's and your own—in a closed and secure cabinet.

- Do not give your Min Pin any medications designed for humans unless your veterinarian prescribes them. Ibuprofen and acetaminophen can be fatal if given to a dog.

- Select toys that are large enough so that your pet cannot swallow them. Toys that can be chewed into pieces can also be swallowed by your dog. Do not give your dog toys made of yarn or string of any kind. (Shoelaces will be attractive to your pet primarily because they hold your scent.)

- Do not have plants that are toxic to dogs in your home or garden. (You can obtain a list of such plants through the American Kennel Club Canine Health Foundation.)

- Keep your Min Pin off a lawn that has been treated with fertilizers or pesticides until after a hard rainfall (even if your lawn service tells you the products are safe). Anything that kills bugs and weeds has to be toxic to some degree.

- If you use insect spray indoors, be sure you keep your Miniature Pinscher out of that room for a few hours after spraying.

- Check with your veterinarian before using any flea or tick spray or dip. Remember, you have a small dog.

- Keep chocolate of all kinds, onions and garlic in closed containers and high cabinets. Your dog can become ill or even die if he eats them.

- Most things that will harm a baby will likewise harm your pet. Keep this in mind when making changes in your home.

Living with
a Miniature
Pinscher

- Monitor your garage floor and driveway for antifreeze drips. Dogs are attracted to it and licking it can be deadly

Finding a Veterinarian

Locating a competent veterinarian is essential to your dog's overall health. If you are moving to a new area, ask your current veterinarian if he or she can recommend someone in your new location. Speak with neighbors who have pets and ask them who they use, and whether they are satisfied with the doctor's services. You can, of course, check the Yellow Pages. Calling your local library and asking for the address of the veterinary association in the state is another choice—they should be able to give you the name of the veterinarian closest to your home.

When choosing a veterinarian, there are several considerations that should impact your decision. Ask yourself the following questions:

- How long has the veterinarian been in practice?
- Does the hospital see many small dogs?
- Is there more than one veterinarian on staff? Does one see more small dogs than the others?
- What is the hospital's policy on after-hour emergencies?
- In a single-doctor practice, what happens when the veterinarian is on vacation or ill?

Once you find what you think is a suitable practice, visit the office. During your visit, ask yourself the following questions:

- Is the veterinary hospital clean?
- Does the hospital seem well equipped?
- Is the staff pleasant and concerned?
- Is the veterinarian gentle with your dog? Does your Min Pin like the veterinarian?
- Is the veterinarian willing to take the time to answer your questions?

66

- Is the veterinarian readily available to answer your calls?

If your dog is ill:

- Does the veterinarian inform you of the diagnosis and why he or she is recommending a particular treatment?
- Are you given the prognosis?
- Is the way to administer the prescribed treatment clearly explained?
- Are you told signs to look for that may necessitate a call back?
- How efficient is the practice in letting you know when your pet is due for routine vaccinations?

BE READY FOR THE VISIT

Treating a pet is often more difficult than treating a person. A Min Pin cannot tell you how he feels, what hurts and whether the treatment is helping. The veterinarian depends on you to provide much of this by observation.

When you move, be sure to request your pet's medical file to give your new veterinarian.

One word of caution: Because many of the dogs visiting a hospital are sick, carry your Min Pin—especially if he is a puppy—to avoid exposure to disease from the floor or the grounds.

Keep a Medical Journal

In today's busy world, it helps to be organized and have all your pet's documents in one safe place. Keeping a detailed medical journal for your dog is highly recommended. You can use a simple three-ring binder with lined pages. Record every visit to your veterinarian, the purpose of the visit and any treatment or tests that were administered or prescribed. The itemized computer bills that most veterinary clinics now provide can be filed in this book along with the proof of vaccinations.

Living with
a Miniature
Pinscher

Whenever your dog has an ailment for which you call your veterinarian, record it with an explanation and the date. The symptoms and recommended treatment should also be included. The strength, dosage, frequency and duration of any medication given should be documented. If you give any of the preventative pills for heartworm, Lyme disease or similar diseases, specify the type and how often you administer it to your pet. Also, include a detailed progress report.

A page to track the various vaccinations administered and the dates on which they were given will provide backup to the veterinarian's records. On this same page, you should monitor your dog's weight by recording it as it is taken by your veterinarian. This will be particularly useful if your dog is overweight. Professional teeth cleaning and surgeries should also be recorded with dates, details and how your pet recovered.

It takes only a few minutes after each visit to keep the journal updated, but it is an indispensable reference for you and anyone else who may be responsible for your dog's care. Should a specific health problem recur and you can't reach your veterinarian, this journal can be helpful in getting treatment started.

You can't always rely on memory to know when your pet needs vaccinations or when his teeth were last cleaned professionally. Having all of this information readily available in one place is invaluable. This type of log will also be very useful if you change your veterinarian or move.

List the names, addresses and phone numbers of the breeder and other dog-related contacts on the back of the binder. Any obedience training classes you have

---

WHEN TO CALL THE VET

In any emergency situation, you should call your veterinarian immediately. You can make the difference in your dog's life by staying as calm as possible when you call and by giving the doctor or the assistant as much information as possible before you leave for the clinic. That way, the vet will be able to take immediate, specific action to remedy your dog's situation.

Emergencies include acute abdominal pain, suspected poisoning, snakebite, burns, frostbite, shock, dehydration, abnormal vomiting or bleeding, and deep wounds. You are the best judge of your dog's health, as you live with and observe him every day. Don't hesitate to call your veterinarian if you suspect trouble.

attended can also be recorded here, including when they were taken and what instructions were provided.

Various documents like the American Kennel Club registration, the pedigree if you were given one, current license and any certificates awarded to your pet (such as Canine Good Citizen) can all be included.

CANINE DISEASES AND VACCINATIONS

Newborn puppies are continuously receiving disease-fighting antibodies from their mother's milk. Once the puppies are weaned, however, the remaining antibodies last for only a short time. For this reason, it is important to know whether or not the breeder has vaccinated your puppy. If the breeder hasn't vaccinated your dog, you must do so immediately. Normally, puppies are given low doses of vaccine at intervals

Keeping your dog's inoculations up to date will help to ensure his good health.

of two to four weeks. Your veterinarian will set up a schedule for your puppy's inoculations. This vaccine is DHLPP, an acronym for the diseases it protects your Miniature Pinscher from contracting. These diseases are discussed in detail below.

Distemper

Canine distemper is a virus that attacks a dog's respiratory, nervous and digestive systems. Early signs are loss of appetite, fever, dehydration, diarrhea, bloody stool, a runny nose and common cold–like symptoms. This virus is airborne and highly contagious.

Hepatitis

Canine hepatitis is a viral infection transmitted through an infected animal's stool, urine or saliva. It is most severe among puppies, affecting their liver and the cells that line their blood vessels. Symptoms are vomiting, diarrhea, abdominal pain, convulsions, hemorrhage and watery eyes.

Leptospirosis

Leptospirosis is a bacterial disease that can cause serious liver and kidney damage and can be fatal. Symptoms include a loss of appetite, lethargy, vomiting, fever, diarrhea and bloody stool, jaundice, mouth ulcers and severe weight loss. This disease also can be communicated from a dog to humans.

Parvovirus

Parvovirus is a highly contagious gastrointestinal virus that strikes without warning. It is transmitted through the secretions of an infected animal and can be fatal, especially in puppies. The first symptom is usually a lack of appetite followed by vomiting, diarrhea, listlessness and dehydration. If treated promptly, the prognosis is good, but if not it can be fatal.

Parainfluenza (Kennel Cough)

Parainfluenza, more commonly known as kennel cough or canine cough, is a viral infection that attacks the respiratory system. Symptoms include a harsh cough, runny nose and eyes, depression and loss of appetite. It is usually not life-threatening, but it can be if it is not treated in the early stages. It can recur or become chronic.

Rabies

Rabies is an infection of the nervous system that affects mammals. Once thought to be almost eradicated, it has recently reappeared in raccoons, foxes, skunks and other wild animals. It is caused by a virus that occurs in the saliva and is spread through the bite of an infected animal. The symptoms of infection include a sensitivity to noise, high excitement and paralysis. If you suspect that your dog has been bitten, contact your veterinarian immediately.

YOUR PUPPY'S VACCINES

Vaccines are given to prevent your dog from getting an infectious disease like canine distemper or rabies. Vaccines are the ultimate preventive medicine: They're given before your dog ever gets the disease so as to protect him from the disease. That's why it is necessary for your dog to be vaccinated routinely. Puppy vaccines start at eight weeks of age for the five-in-one DHLPP vaccine and are given every three to four weeks until the puppy is sixteen months old. Your veterinarian will put your puppy on a proper schedule and will remind you when to bring in your dog for shots.

The vaccination for rabies is administered separately from the other vaccinations discussed, usually when the puppy is three to six months old. It is repeated in one year and then given either annually or every three years.

Parasites

A number of parasites, both external (usually living on the skin of your dog) and internal (parasites that usually reside in the intestines, stomach, heart and other internal organs) live off of your dog. It is important to watch out for them, as they are both a nuisance and a health hazard.

EXTERNAL PARASITES

Fleas

Fleas can be visible on a Miniature Pinscher coat, or they can be seen jumping on or off your dog. These small pests are fast and difficult to capture. They inhabit grass and can be brought in to your house via your dog no matter how meticulously both he and your home are kept. Fleas leave black specks—their waste products—on the dog's skin. These droppings are the clearest indication of the presence of fleas on the dog.

Fleas will irritate your dog, causing him to scratch. Other indications of an infestation are anemia and in some cases, weight loss. Fleas carry tapeworm eggs which your Miniature Pinscher might ingest, causing infection. (Tapeworms are discussed later in this chapter.)

> **FIGHTING FLEAS**
>
> Remember, the fleas you see on your dog are only part of the problem—the smallest part! To rid your dog and home of fleas, you need to treat your dog *and* your home. Here's how:
>
> • Identify where your pet(s) sleep. These are "hot spots."
>
> • Clean your pets' bedding regularly by vacuuming and washing.
>
> • Spray "hot spots" with a non-toxic, long-lasting flea larvicide.
>
> • Treat outdoor "hot spots" with insecticide.
>
> • Kill eggs on pets with a product containing insect growth regulators (IGRs).
>
> • Kill fleas on pets per your veterinarian's recommendation.

Before you buy a flea collar, consult with your veterinarian. Flea collars can be toxic—some dogs are allergic to them and children should not be permitted to

touch them. If a dog that is wearing a flea collar needs
to be anesthetized for emergency surgery, there is
potential for serious respiratory complications. In addition, elective surgery requires removal of the collar
two weeks prior to the operation.

Some collars are made from natural eucalyptus, and
these are safe. Brewer's yeast taken internally can be
used as a natural short-term deterrent to these pests.

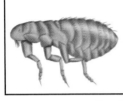

Fleas also dislike the scent of Skin So Soft™ by
Avon. This product can be diluted and sprayed
on your Min Pin's coat as a repellent.

Combing your Miniature Pinscher often with a
fine-toothed comb can dislodge fleas. You can
then quickly pick them off with tweezers and
dip the tweezers with the flea into a small container
filled with alcohol.

*The flea is a
die-hard pest.*

*Use tweezers to
remove ticks
from your dog.*

You can easily trap a flea, should you spot one, by pressing the fur down with your finger and using the tweezers with your other hand to capture it. Dispose of it
quickly in the alcohol, making certain it's deep into

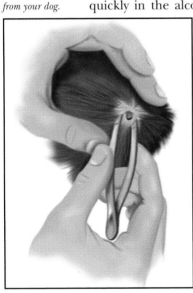

the container (remember—fleas
can jump!).

Some Miniature Pinschers are
allergic to fleas and will chew at
their skin until it is raw. Should
this occur, or if your dog does not
have a reaction but is obviously
infested with fleas, consult your
veterinarian.

Ticks

Ticks bury their heads into a
dog's skin and feed on his blood.
They gorge themselves to at least
twice their size and can be readily
seen when they are enlarged.
They inhabit woods and sandy beaches. Ticks are car-
riers of Lyme disease and Rocky Mountain Spotted
Fever and are a health hazard to both dogs and
humans.

Examining your dog, using both your eyes and your hands, will enable you to locate a tick. First, with a piece of cotton or cotton swab soaked in alcohol, thoroughly wet the tick and the area around it. After a minute, it should release its hold, and you can remove

it with tweezers or a plastic device designed for this purpose. Plastic tick removers are available in some pet supply shops or at your veterinarian's office. These removers

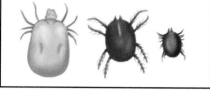

look like a small spoon with a groove to lift off the tick. Be sure you fully remove the head, as it can cause infection if it is left on the skin.

Three types of ticks (l-r): the wood tick, brown dog tick and deer tick.

INTERNAL PARASITES

Heartworm

Heartworms are transmitted through the bite of infected mosquitoes. These parasites eventually settle in the dog's heart. Blood tests can determine the presence of the microfilaria (larvae) in the blood, indicating that your dog probably has adult worms. Preven-tative medication is available, as well as remedial treatment if your dog already has heartworms. The treatment does involve some possible side effects, which your veterinarian will explain. Your dog should be tested for heartworms annually. It's vital that your dog be tested prior to the start of taking a preventative. If your dog is infected at the time he is administered a preventative, the medicine will kill the heartworms but can also cause circulatory blockage or even result in death.

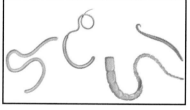

Common internal parasites (l-r): roundworm, whipworm, tapeworm and hookworm.

Hookworm

As its name implies, the hookworm attaches itself to a dog's small intestine. Symptoms include loss of appetite, a dark or bloody stool, listlessness and anemia. In addition, the membranes of the mouth of an infected dog are sometimes very pale.

73

Roundworm

Roundworms are sometimes seen in your dog's stool. Puppies are more likely than adult dogs to get them, and the condition can be serious if it's not treated. These worms are long and light and resemble spaghetti. The larvae travel through the puppy's system causing vomiting, diarrhea and, at times, pneumonia. When you see them in your dog's stool, they will be curled up in a circle. If you think your dog may be infected with roundworms, consult your veterinarian. Treatment is usually very successful.

Tapeworm

The larva of the tapeworm enters the dog's body by way of a flea. Segments of the tapeworm are sometimes visible in the dog's feces. Except for some weight loss, there are no other symptoms. Your veterinarian can recommend treatment.

Whipworm

Whipworm causes mucus in the stool, bowel inflammation and diarrhea. Whipworms are microscopic, and so an infection cannot be detected with the naked eye even through close observation. Your veterinarian should prescribe treatment for the specific internal parasite your dog may have.

When Should You Call a Veterinarian?

A difficult decision for an owner is under what circumstances one should call the vet. Most often, the indications are clear when professional help is required. But there are borderline situations that require an owner's judgment. When in doubt, err on the side of caution and call your veterinarian.

INDICATIONS

No one knows your Miniature Pinscher better than you do. Likewise, no one knows better what constitutes normal behavior and habits for your dog like you do. There may be some obvious visual signs such as lameness, vomiting, swelling, persistent licking, constipation, diarrhea or a dramatic change in coat condition. All of these, if not severe, should be monitored. If these problems persist, they will require veterinary care.

Make sure that your dog is active—exercise is as important for dogs as it is for people.

Refusal to eat or go out, lethargy, whimpering, restlessness or any abnormal behavior should be recorded and reported to your veterinarian when you decide to call. Examine your dog to try to find the reason for the problem. For example, lameness may be caused by a pebble being caught between your dog's pads, a cut on the foot, or a bur or splinter. Check the body for sore spots. Your pet will usually pull away or cry out if you touch a tender area. If some part of the body is hot to the touch, it is normally a sign of infection.

Run your hands regularly over your dog to feel for any injuries.

CHECKING YOUR DOG'S TEMPERATURE

You will want to check your dog's temperature before calling the veterinarian. Lubricate the end of a rectal thermometer with petroleum jelly. Holding your Min Pin securely (get a family member to help if necessary), carefully insert the thermometer about an inch into the anus. It takes about two minutes to obtain an accurate reading. Some of the newer, digital thermometers chime when finished. A dog's temperature should be 101.5°F—the normal range is 100.0 to 102.5°F. A young puppy's temperature is slightly lower. Always clean the thermometer with cotton or a tissue and alcohol to prevent spreading disease.

CHECKING YOUR DOG'S PULSE

Take your Min Pin's pulse. Lay your hand just behind the dog's shoulder blade on either side of the chest and find his heartbeat. Count the number of beats per minute (or count for fifteen seconds and then multiply the beats by four). Another method is to place your hand in the groin of the dog, near the abdomen, and feel for a pulse. The normal range is from 100 to 125 beats per minute. If the dog is upset or excited, the pulse can be considerably higher. Record the pulse rate and the time it was taken. This information can assist your veterinarian in diagnosis.

Signs of Possible Illness

Once you know your Miniature Pinscher, you usually know when something is wrong. Early detection can greatly facilitate an early cure. Running your hands over your dog's body to detect anything unusual at the same time each day will help. Try to do this at a time that's convenient for you. It will eventually become part of your everyday routine.

Some signs that your dog is sick are listed below. If any of these problems occur, be sure to contact your veterinarian.

- Breathing difficulty
- Blood in urine
- Loss of appetite or weight
- A dull coat or profuse shedding
- Change in bowel habits, constipation or diarrhea

- Foul odors emitted from ears, mouth or any other body part

- Increased water intake

- Incessant scratching or biting of the skin

- Lameness or hesitation in climbing or descending stairs

- Lethargy or depression

- Skin lesions, any swelling, lumps or growths

- Soreness or tenderness anywhere on the body

- Vomiting or dry heaves

- Persistent cough

In addition to the warning signs listed above, always monitor your dog's weight closely. Extra weight creates the same health hazards in dogs it does in humans. Dogs can develop heart problems, diabetes, digestive system disorders and lung disease. An overweight dog puts extra stress on the skeletal frame, and obesity can lead to arthritis and other problems. Please refer to chapter 5 on nutrition for reducing the weight of an obese dog.

First Aid for Your Dog

A first-aid kit is essential for your Min Pin as well as your human family. It will ensure that you have quick, easy access to the necessary supplies should a canine emergency occur. In addition to the items listed in the accompanying sidebar, make sure that your kit includes a card containing the telephone numbers of your veterinarian's

---

A FIRST-AID KIT

Keep a canine first-aid kit on hand for general care and emergencies. Check it periodically to make sure liquids haven't spilled or dried up, and replace medications and materials after they're used. Your kit should include:

Activated charcoal tablets to absorb poison

Adhesive tape
(1 and 2 inches wide)

Antibacterial ointment
(for skin and eyes)

Aspirin (buffered or enteric coated, *not* Ibuprofen)

Bandages: Gauze rolls (1 and 2 inches wide) and dressing pads

Cotton balls

Diarrhea medicine

Dosing syringe

Hydrogen peroxide (3%)

Petroleum jelly

Rectal thermometer

Rubber gloves

Rubbing alcohol

Scissors

Tourniquet

Towel

Tweezers

office, the nearest 24-hour emergency veterinary hospital and your local poison control center.

Be sure everyone in the family knows where the first-aid kit is located. Take it with you on outings or vacations. You may even want a smaller version to keep in your car. Periodically check to see that the supplies are not outdated and replace those that are.

Administering First Aid

Prevention is always the best way to handle a medical situation. Be aware of hazards to which your pet might be exposed, and take the necessary precautions *before* something happens. In the event of an emergency, however, first aid may be essential.

Take a first-aid kit along when you bring your dogs on an outing.

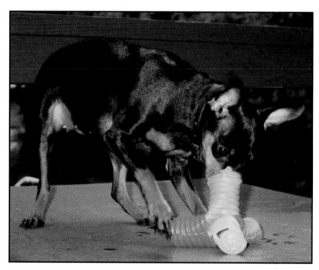

First aid is just that—a way to aid you in giving immediate treatment in emergencies until veterinary care can be obtained. Preparing a first-aid kit and having it readily available will enable you to give your dog the best chance for recovery from a medical emergency. Time is critical.

MUZZLING A MINIATURE PINSCHER

Even the most placid dog may try to bite out of fear or pain. An injured dog should be muzzled (except if he's vomiting or having trouble breathing) before being treated. If you don't have a muzzle, a nylon stocking, scarf or doubled-up piece of gauze can all be used. Wrap the fabric twice around the muzzle, bring the ends back and tie the ends firmly at the back of the neck. The dog will probably object, especially if the muzzle is too tight. It should be secured just tight enough to prevent the Min Pin from being able to use his jaws to bite, but no tighter.

Use a scarf or old hose to make a temporary muzzle, as shown.

BEE STINGS AND INSECT BITES

If your dog is stung, apply ice, wrapped in a small towel, to the painful, swollen area. Remove the stinger (if it is visible) with tweezers. An antihistamine like Benadryl™ can be given. Be sure to administer the lowest child's dosage. A saline solution can be applied to the infected area. If your pet appears to be in shock, has breathing problems or the swelling worsens, call your veterinarian at once.

BLEEDING

If your dog is bleeding, apply direct pressure to the wound using a gauze pad or any clean cloth. If you have rolled gauze, place it over the wound and tie it tightly over the pad or cloth. A belt, dog's lead or anything similar that you have on hand can be used to tie the pad in place. If this doesn't reduce the bleeding, apply a tourniquet between the heart and the wound. Remove the tourniquet as soon as the bleeding stops. Release the tour-niquet every five minutes to see if the bleeding has stopped. Prolonged use of a tourniquet can have serious consequences. Seek a veterinarian's help quickly.

BREATHING DIFFICULTY

*Applying
abdominal
thrusts can save
a choking dog.*

If your Miniature Pinscher has trouble breathing, or if his gums and tongue are turning blue, artificial respiration is needed. Place the Min Pin on a flat surface, preferably at table height, extend the head and neck. Pull the tongue gently, and using your finger check the throat for obstructions. Place your mouth over the dog's nose and mouth to form a seal and exhale until the dog's chest expands. Release until the chest goes down. Repeat at intervals of twelve to fifteen breaths per minute until the Min Pin is able to breathe on his own. Consult your veterinarian im-mediately to follow up.

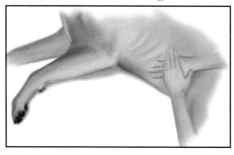

BURNS

If your dog is burned by fire or heat, rinse the affected area with large amounts of cool water.

If the problem is the result of a chemical burn, shampoo the area, leaving the lather on for several minutes, and then rinse several times with clear water. A saline solution can be applied, and the affected area should be covered with antibiotic ointment.

An acid burn can be treated with a paste of one part baking soda and two parts water. On an alkali burn, use a vinegar solution of one part vinegar and four parts water.

An electric burn should be treated with antibiotic ointment. Be aware that if the dog has received an electric shock, heart damage may have resulted.

Burns can become infected and cause your pet to become dehydrated. Always consult your veterinarian for assistance.

CAR ACCIDENT

Immediate care is crucial if your Min Pin is hit by a vehicle. In addition to the physical trauma, a dog that has been hit by a car can go into shock. If your dog is having trouble breathing, keep him in an upright position. Be sure to muzzle your dog before treating him, *except* if he is vomiting or experiencing breathing problems. Keep your Min Pin as still as possible. You may need to wrap your dog in a towel. Speak to your dog in a calm, reassuring way to ease the fright. If your dog is bleeding, apply pressure to the wound with a gauze pad or clean cloth (refer to "Bleeding" above). Get your dog to a veterinarian *right away*.

 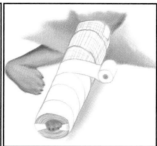

Make a temporary splint by wrapping the leg in firm casing, then bandaging it.

DIARRHEA

Diarrhea can have numerous causes. Dietary changes, intestinal parasites, a virus, and ingestion of poisons, toxic plants or harmful foods such as chocolate or onions can all be cited as the reasons for this problem.

Kaopectate™ administered by an eyedropper or dosage syringe can be given if the dog's diet has been changed. Feeding plain cooked rice and boiled chicken or hamburger meat for a day or so may help. If the diarrhea is watery, bloody or foul smelling, or if you don't know what is causing it, consult a veterinarian promptly.

Some of the many household substances harmful to your dog.

DROWNING

If your dog has almost drowned, hold him by his hind legs upside down to drain any water from his airway. Gently tapping the chest may speed fluid removal.

Then lay the dog on his side. Check to see if he is breathing and then check for a pulse. If the dog is not breathing, follow the artificial respiration instructions under "Breathing Difficulty" above. If there is either no pulse or only a faint pulse, get another person to press a hand just behind the dog's shoulder blade. It should be a firm but gentle compression. If you are alone, alternate between breathing and applying compression. Continue to check for a pulse and breathing. As with any other emergency condition, seek immediate veterinary help.

Transporting an Injured Dog to the Veterinarian

A crate or sturdy cardboard box lined with a towel or blanket can be used to transport an injured Min Pin. Gently place your Min Pin in by sliding your hand under him and supporting his entire body when lifting. Obviously, the injured area should be exposed. Place towels around to keep your pet from being shifted during travel.

When Your Pet Needs Medication

WHEN ADMINISTERING ANY MEDICATION

- Use the exact dosage prescribed and give it on the correct schedule.

- Ask your veterinarian if there are any side effects, such as increased thirst.

- Ask your veterinarian whether it matters if the medication is given before or after meals, or if it should be given between meals.

- Do not give a drug prescribed for one pet to another unless your veterinarian tells you to do so.

- Ask your veterinarian if you can discontinue the medication if your pet improves. Certain medications, like antibiotics, must be given for a certain term, even if the dog seems healthy again.

PILLS

There are some ways to simplify giving your pet medication prescribed by the veterinarian. A tablet or capsule can be wrapped in cheese (cream cheese works best) or meat (liverwurst is favored) and offered to the dog. Actually, any food that your dog likes in which the pill can be placed should do the trick. If your pet doesn't take it, hold his mouth open with one hand and with the other, using your index finger, quickly deposit the pill on the middle of the tongue as far back as you can. Hold your dog's mouth closed while stroking his throat to encourage swallowing. Be sure that the pill has gone down before releasing the jaw.

To give a pill, open the mouth wide, then place it in the back of the throat.

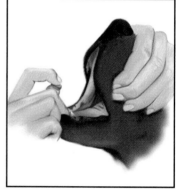

LIQUID MEDICATIONS

When administering liquid medication, use a syringe or eye dropper which is scored to show measurements. Fill the syringe with the prescribed dosage, hold open the dog's lower lip on the side and place the end of the syringe between the cheek and gums. Release the liquid, quickly close the mouth and hold the muzzle until the medication is swallowed.

Putting the liquid into the dog's food is not a good idea. He may be turned off by the odor or the taste and refuse to eat altogether or may just eat around the medication.

EAR MEDICATIONS

Ear medications usually come with a long, thin nozzle that enables you to apply the medication well into the ear canal. Your Min Pin may object, so to prevent him from getting away, hold him firmly with your arm over him, use the hand on the holding arm to steady the ear while you put the ointment into the ear with the other hand. Then, gently massage the ear.

EYE MEDICATIONS

*Squeeze eye oint-
ment into the
lower lid.*

Liquid eye medicine can be given by using a dropper and placing the appropriate number of drops into the corner of the eye. Ointments can be applied by pulling down the lower eyelid and placing the medicine directly on it. Close the eye gently and hold it closed

for a minute to distribute the medicine over the entire eye.

It helps to give your dog a treat and compliment him for being good (even if he didn't cooperate) after the medication is administered. Your pet may accept the procedure more readily the next time.

If Your Min Pin Is Hospitalized

If your dog is hospitalized, you will have to make sure that you have prepared correctly. The following is a checklist of things that need to be done to make sure that your dog has a safe stay in the hospital:

- Leave a scented towel, blanket or a piece of your clothing with your dog to help him feel more secure. A favorite toy will also console your canine.

- Ask what treatment will be administered, if they know how long your dog will need to be hospitalized and if they are able to make a diagnosis at that point.

- Advise the staff of all symptoms and changes you have observed and if your dog has any special needs or problems or any unusual habits. Even if the veterinarian prescribed the medication that your pet is on, it helps to remind the staff so it's not overlooked.

- Leave a telephone number where you or a family member can be reached at all times, should the veterinarian have questions or need to discuss treatment.

- Determine the best time to call for progress reports and whether you can visit your Min Pin during his confinement if you wish.

- Inquire about charges in advance if you have financial concerns. Some tests are costly and you may want to ask if they are necessary or optional. Your veterinarian should know what you are able to spend. Most veterinarians are cooperative about telling you the anticipated costs, but some can present you with astronomical bills exceeding your expectations. It's best when there are no surprises. At the very least, expressing your concern will alert the veterinarian that you would like costs to be discussed with you *beforehand.*

- If the expense is not a problem and the condition serious, ask if the pet should be seen by a specialist. Referral clinics are becoming increasingly available.

- When you bring your pet home, the veterinarian will usually provide you with information on any special care required. Ask when your dog has eaten and been exercised last. If medication is prescribed, find out when it should be given. Are there any side effects? Ask if you should be alert to any differences in behavior or in the dog's condition.

An Elizabethan collar keeps your dog from licking a fresh wound.

- What is the prognosis? Will the condition be likely to recur?

- If your Min Pin has had surgery, ask when the sutures should come out or if they will dissolve. Your veterinarian may recommend that your dog wear an Elizabethan collar while his wounds heal.

- Does your veterinarian want you to report back; and if so, when? Is a follow-up visit required or only if certain symptoms occur?

FOLLOW-UPS

Your Min Pin will do best if you take responsibility in his medical care along with your veterinarian. Your veterinarian will also be aware of how much you are concerned about your pet's health.

Don't trust your questions or concerns to memory. Make a written list of things that you feel should be discussed with your veterinarian or the staff whenever you visit or talk on the phone.

Spaying or Neutering Your Pet

Spaying or neutering your Miniature Pinscher helps to assure that your pet will live a healthier and longer life.

THE SPAYED FEMALE

A spayed female is spared possible cancer of the reproductive organs and is at less risk of having mammary tumors, going through false pregnancy or coming down with pyometrea, a serious uterine infection. *You* are spared the staining problems of a female in heat (heat usually lasts three weeks and occurs between every six months and one year). Female dogs come into season throughout their lives. You will not be visited by neighborhood males attracted by her scent and will not have to manage an unwanted litter.

THE NEUTERED MALE

A neutered male has a lower risk of prostate or anal cancer, and neutering totally eliminates the possibility of testicular cancer. The male is less likely to roam, and his association with other male dogs will be greatly improved.

ADVANTAGES OF SPAY/NEUTER

The greatest advantage of spaying (for females) or neutering (for males) your dog is that you are guaranteed your dog will not produce puppies. There are too many puppies already available for too few homes. There are other advantages as well.

ADVANTAGES OF SPAYING

No messy heats.

No "suitors" howling at your windows or waiting in your yard.

Decreased incidences of pyometra (disease of the uterus) and breast cancer.

ADVANTAGES OF NEUTERING

Lessens male aggressive and territorial behaviors, but doesn't affect the dog's personality. Behaviors are often owner-induced, so neutering is not the only answer, but it is a good start.

Prevents the need to roam in search of bitches in season.

Decreased incidences of urogenital diseases.

There's no question that both altered males and females are emotionally happier, physically healthier and make better companions.

Just as importantly, we are faced with a very serious pet overpopulation problem in many parts of the country, and the world. Thousands of dogs are euthanized in shelters annually. Others live unfortunate lives, as strays often meeting difficult deaths from starvation or disease.

WHY TO NOT BREED

Shelters are receiving an increased number of pure-bred dogs. With the popularity of Miniature Pinschers escalating, our rescue coordinators are being called to help place Min Pins with increasing frequency.

Professional and hobby breeders will only breed their best dogs, test for hereditary health problems, study pedigrees, and have the expertise to care properly for the pregnant female and the puppies. The responsibilities of breeding are best left in the hands of those who have the knowledge, time and resources to do so correctly.

Alternative Medical Treatment

Traditional medical treatment is based primarily on drugs and surgery. There is a growing trend toward alternative and holistic medicine in the veterinary field today. Acupuncture, herbal remedies, massage, chiropractic treatment and homeopathy are just some of the methods offered by an increasing number of veterinarians. These veterinarians focus heavily on the preventative approach to health care as well as new avenues of treatment previously not available for canines.

There are several excellent books on this trend worth reading. I highly suggest *Love, Miracles and Animal Healing,* by Allen M. Schoen, DVM and Pam Proctor, Simon and Schuster (1995), and *Keep Your Pet Healthy* the Natural Way, by Pat Lazarus, A Keat/Pivot Health Book (1986), Macmillan edition (1983). Any course of therapy you consider should be discussed with your veterinarian.

Breeders do the best they can to control canine genetic diseases.

Health Problems Occurring Frequently in the Miniature Pinscher

Most breeds have health problems to which they are particularly susceptible. While on the whole Miniature Pinschers are a sturdy and healthy breed, certain maladies do exist. It's best to question the breeder from whom you get your dog about any problems in that dog's line. Most conscientious breeders will volunteer any medical concerns in the ancestry, so you and your veterinarian can monitor your pet for these maladies.

LEGG-CALVE PERTHES DISEASE

Legg-Calve Perthes Disease is a problem of the hip and is named after the three men who independently identified the difficulty with children's hips in 1910. This disease is caused by impaired blood supply to the femoral head and is normally found in small breeds whose members weigh less than twenty pounds. The onset age varies, but it is usually before one year with a peak incidence during about seven months of age. The cause is unknown, and it usually occurs only on one leg.

A Min Pin suffering from this disease will usually limp and show pain when his leg is extended or rotated. A positive diagnosis is made by X-ray. Treatment is surgical resection or removal of the femoral head. The best results are obtained if the surgery is performed before the onset of arthritis.

MANGE

Mange is caused by microscopic mites of two varieties: demodectic and sarcoptic. *Demodectic mange* is the more common in Miniature Pinschers and causes patches of hair loss, often on the face but also elsewhere on the body. It is more common in puppies and, because dogs have a natural immunity to mites, is believed to be brought on by stress or some other condition that weakens the immune system.

At times, this condition can cause the loss of coat over large sections of the dog's body. It can be diagnosed by your veterinarian taking a skin scraping and examining it under a microscope. The condition is treated with medical dips performed by a veterinarian.

Sarcoptic mange is contagious and often covers more of the dog's body. The loss of fur is generally more extensive than with demodectic mange. Medicated dips are formulated to kill both parasites. If baths are given at home, you should wear rubber gloves because the medication contains substances to kill the mites.

ANAL GLANDS

Min Pins tend to get impacted anal glands or sacs, which can cause considerable irritation. If your dog is scooting around the floor on his backside, you may need to have his anal glands cleaned.

The anal glands can be expressed by using a tissue and placing your forefinger and thumb in the 4 o'clock and 8 o'clock positions on either side of the anus.

Hold your Min Pin securely while exerting pressure with your thumb and finger. You should be able to empty the sacs. Usually the waste is liquid, but it can harden. Ask your veterinarian to show you how to do this procedure.

At times the glands will abscess and form a fissure. Warm water Epsom™ salt compresses will offer relief until you get to the veterinarian. The abscess may rupture and drain, and this will usually leave a scar. Your veterinarian may prescribe an antibiotic if an abscess forms.

DIABETES

Diabetes sometimes occurs in Min Pins that are overweight and is most often seen in older dogs. Excess drinking is a common symptom. This may be accompanied by loss of weight. Certain lines seem more predisposed to this problem than others. Treatment consists of giving your dog insulin injections, as oral medication for diabetes is not effective with dogs. Your veterinarian will train you in how to monitor glucose levels and administer the insulin intravenously. Periodic professional medical checks are normally required to keep the dosage regulated.

SENSITIVITY TO LEPTOSPIROSIS VACCINE

Some Miniature Pinschers are allergic to a component in the inoculation for leptospirosis. Right after your pet receives this vaccine, which is given to puppies and adults throughout life, your Min Pin should be carefully observed for hives, swelling (this usually occurs on the face) or breathing problems. Should these symptoms occur, contact your veterinarian at once so that an antidote can be administered.

DENTAL HYGIENE

Since most toy dogs have a predisposition to dental problems, special attention should be given to your Miniature Pinscher's teeth. Ask your veterinarian to check your dog's teeth each time you visit. Follow his or her recommendations on periodic professional cleaning and follow the instructions on dental care as outlined in chapter 6. Prevention is the key, and good dental hygiene is a must.

Plaque buildup is common; and it leads to tartar. Tartar is an accumulation of dead cells and bacteria that becomes a hard coating on the teeth. If not removed, it can lead to gingivitis, indications of which include an inflammation of the gums and abscesses. Neglect can also cause osteomyelitis, an infection of the bone. When plaque first forms, it is soft and can easily be removed by brushing, scraping with your thumb nail and by giving your dog hard foods to chew on.

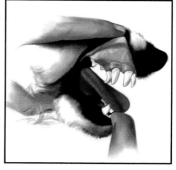

Veterinary dentistry has become quite sophisticated in recent years. Root canals, curettage (scraping gum tissue around teeth), implants—almost all services available for humans are being offered for dogs. Periodontal disease is a very serious dental problem in dogs and can cause serious diseases related to the heart and other organs.

Check your dog's teeth frequently and brush them regularly.

Love Is the Best Medicine

Any health problem your Min Pin may have can be aided with a generous dose of love. Proponents of the mind-body connection stress the importance of the dog's emotional state in the healing process. These advocates have provided some valid and extensive evidence that the will to live can cure. Likewise, and particularly with dogs as sensitive as Min Pins, if they are loved and leading a content life, there is no stronger medicine.

The Geriatric Miniature Pinscher

There are steps that you can take to provide the best quality of life for your Miniature Pinscher in his advanced years. First, the many senior diets will be better suited to your pet's nutritional needs. Exercise is as important as ever, if not more so, but should be moderate to accommodate your pet's physical capabilities. As usual, consistency is the key. Often, Miniature Pinschers will be surprisingly active through their advanced years. Older dogs, like older people, usually prefer warmth. A softer bed will make your Min Pin's aging bones and joints more comfortable, and added covers will be welcome for warmth. Younger pets and active children can wear on an older dog's nerves. Try to minimize these annoyances to the degree possible.

At this stage of life, more than ever before, your pet needs attention and tenderness. The kind words, a warm lap, stroking and an occasional massage will help his emotional health tremendously and prolong his life. Your loving gestures will be relished, and your Min Pin will show appreciation by returning your love in abundance.

Don't neglect routine medical visits in your pet's geriatric years. Early detection and treatment of age-related potential problems can prevent them from advancing to more serious levels. Consistent care of the teeth and gums is critical, and your dog may need to have some teeth pulled, as diseased teeth cause gum inflammation and infection leading to complications. Keeping the nails short will reduce the discomfort associated with arthritis to a minimum.

Monitor your dog's water intake diligently. Increased thirst might indicate the onset of diabetes or kidney malfunction. Your veterinarian is best equipped to make these years enjoyable for your Min Pin, but you can play a major role in helping him or her do this. Alert your veterinarian of any changes in your pet that may have medical significance.

MEDICAL PROBLEMS AFFECTING AGING DOGS

Because Min Pins live a long time, problems that come along with age sometimes develop. These problems are frequently associated with the dog's eyes and ears.

Sight

Failing vision, cataracts or glaucoma and occasionally blindness may occur. A veterinary ophthalmologist can offer treatments which may include daily eye drops for glaucoma in order to relieve pressure and surgery for cataracts.

With decreasing vision, it's important to keep the physical aspects of your dog's environment relatively the same. Even blind Min Pins do incredibly well in getting around, but you may have to use safety gates at stairways and block off areas where the dog can fall.

Blind dogs become more sensitive to sound. You might find that you are able to clap your hands to call a blind dog, and that he will quickly respond. We found, with one of our Min Pins, that she naturally assumed the role of a seeing-eye dog and would "herd" the blind dog by going from side to side and steering her blind companion to the door. It was amazing to watch.

Hearing

Hearing can diminish with advancing years as well. Most noticeably, your Miniature Pinscher may not come when summoned or hear you when you come home.

Should your dog become deaf, extra caution will be required when he is exposed to cars and other dangers during a walk to protect him. As with a loss of eyesight, dogs adapt extremely well to this handicap. You just have to know to give it visible rather than vocal signals. Dogs that have been trained in obedience to respond to hand signals benefit greatly and adjust easily to being deaf. A method of teaching sign language to deaf dogs is being developed with surprisingly positive results.

SAYING GOODBYE

Eventually, all living things die. We are fortunate to have a long-lived breed and can enjoy our companions for a few years longer than owners of some other breeds. While it is a difficult choice, when a dog's life reaches a point where he is in constant pain and suffering due to severe illness or old age, we have the option to end his misery.

This is a difficult, painful decision and one which should be made jointly by the veterinarian and the owner. The last kindness you can do for your pet is to hold and stroke him while a lethal, painless injection is administered. Some veterinarians recommend giving your pet a strong sedative at home and then taking the dog to the veterinary clinic, while asleep, for euthanasia.

Losing a pet creates an enormous void in the life of the owner. There are now support groups in many cities and excellent books have been written to help the owner through this difficult time. Take advantage of the help available.

Your Happy, Healthy Pet

Your Dog's Name _____

Name on Your Dog's Pedigree (if your dog has one) _____

_____

Where Your Dog Came From _____

_____

Your Dog's Birthday _____

Your Dog's Veterinarian

    Name _____

    Address _____

    Phone Number_____

    Emergency Number_____

Your Dog's Health

    Vaccines

    type _____ date given _____

    type _____ date given _____

    type _____ date given _____

    type _____ date given _____

    Heartworm

    date tested _____ type used_____ start date _____

Your Dog's License Number_____

Groomer's Name and Number _____

Dogsitter/Walker's Name and Number_____

Awards Your Dog Has Won

    Award _____ date earned _____

    Award _____ date earned _____

part three

Enjoying
your
Dog

chapter 8

Basic
Training

by Ian Dunbar, Ph.D., MRCVS

Training is the jewel in the crown—the most important aspect of doggy husbandry. There is no more important variable influencing dog behavior and temperament than the dog's education: A well-trained, well-behaved and good-natured puppydog is always a joy to live with, but an untrained and uncivilized dog can be a perpetual nightmare. Moreover, deny the dog an education and she will not have the opportunity to fulfill her own canine potential; neither will she have the ability to communicate effectively with her human companions.

Luckily, modern psychological training methods are easy, efficient, effective and, above all, considerably dog-friendly and user-friendly.

Doggy education is as simple as it is enjoyable. But before you can have a good time play-training with your new dog, you have to learn what to do and how to do it. There is no bigger variable influencing the success of dog training than the *owner's* experience and expertise. *Before you embark on the dog's education, you must first educate yourself.*

Basic Training for Owners

Ideally, basic owner training should begin well *before* you select your dog. Find out all you can about your chosen breed first, then master rudimentary training and handling skills. If you already have your puppy-dog, owner training is a dire emergency—the clock is ticking! Especially for puppies, the first few weeks at home are the most important and influential days in the dog's life. Indeed, the cause of most adolescent and adult problems may be traced back to the initial days the pup explores her new home. This is the time to establish the *status quo*—to teach the puppydog how you would like her to behave and so prevent otherwise quite predictable problems.

In addition to consulting breeders and breed books such as this one (which understandably have a positive breed bias), seek out as many pet owners with your breed as you can find. Good points are obvious. What you want to find out are the breed-specific *problems,* so you can nip them in the bud. In particular, you should talk to owners with *adolescent* dogs and make a list of all anticipated problems. Most important, *test drive* at least half a dozen adolescent and adult dogs of your breed yourself. An 8-week-old puppy is deceptively easy to handle, but she will acquire adult size, speed and strength in just four months, so you should learn now what to prepare for.

Puppy and pet dog training classes offer a convenient venue to locate pet owners and observe dogs in action. For a list of suitable trainers in your area, contact the Association of Pet Dog Trainers (see chapter 13). You may also begin your basic owner training by observing other owners in class. Watch as many classes and test drive as many dogs as possible. Select an upbeat, dog-friendly, people-friendly, fun-and-games, puppydog pet training class to learn the ropes. Also, watch training videos and read training books. You must find out what to do and how to do it *before* you have to do it.

Principles of Training

Most people think training comprises teaching the dog to do things such as sit, speak and roll over, but even a 4-week-old pup knows how to do these things already. Instead, the first step in training involves teaching the dog human words for each dog behavior and activity and for each aspect of the dog's environment. That way you, the owner, can more easily participate in the dog's domestic education by directing her to perform specific actions appropriately, that is, at the right time, in the right place and so on. Training opens communication channels, enabling an educated dog to at least understand her owner's requests.

In addition to teaching a dog *what* we want her to do, it is also necessary to teach her *why* she should do what we ask. Indeed, 95 percent of training revolves around motivating the dog *to want to do* what we want. Dogs often understand what their owners want; they just don't see the point of doing it—especially when the owner's repetitively boring and seemingly senseless instructions are totally at odds with much more pressing and exciting doggy distractions. It is not so much the dog that is being stubborn or dominant; rather, it is the owner who has failed to acknowledge the dog's needs and feelings and to approach training from the dog's point of view.

THE MEANING OF INSTRUCTIONS

The secret to successful training is learning how to use training lures to predict or prompt specific behaviors—to coax the dog to do what you want *when* you want. Any highly valued object (such as a treat or toy) may be used as a lure, which the dog will follow with her eyes and nose. Moving the lure in specific ways entices the dog to move her nose, head and entire body in specific ways. In fact, by learning the art of manipulating various lures, it is possible to teach the dog to assume virtually any body position and perform any action. Once you have control over the expression of the dog's behaviors and can elicit any body position or behavior at will, you can easily teach the dog to perform on request.

Tell your dog what you want her to do, use a lure to entice her to respond correctly, then profusely praise and maybe reward her once she performs the desired action. For example, verbally request "Tina, sit!" while you move a squeaky toy upwards and backwards over the dog's muzzle (lure-movement and hand signal), smile knowingly as she looks up (to follow the lure) and sits down (as a result of canine anatomical engineering), then praise her to distraction ("Gooood Tina!"). Squeak the toy, offer a training treat and give your dog and yourself a pat on the back.

Being able to elicit desired responses over and over enables the owner to reward the dog over and over. Consequently, the dog begins to think training is fun. For example, the more the dog is rewarded for sitting, the more she enjoys sitting. Eventually the dog comes to realize that, whereas most sitting is appreciated, sitting immediately upon request usually prompts especially enthusiastic praise and a slew of high-level rewards. The dog begins to sit on cue much of the time, showing that she is starting to grasp the meaning of the owner's verbal request and hand signal.

WHY COMPLY?

Most dogs enjoy initial lure-reward training and are only too happy to comply with their owners' wishes. Unfortunately, repetitive drilling without appreciative feedback tends to diminish the dog's enthusiasm until she eventually fails to see the point of complying anymore. Moreover, as the dog approaches adolescence she becomes more easily distracted as she develops other interests. Lengthy sessions with repetitive exercises tend to bore and demotivate both parties. If it's not fun, the owner doesn't do it and neither does the dog.

Integrate training into your dog's life: The greater number of training sessions each day and the *shorter* they are, the more willingly compliant your dog will

become. Make sure to have a short (just a few seconds) training interlude before every enjoyable canine activity. For example, ask your dog to sit to greet people, to sit before you throw her Frisbee and to sit for her supper. Really, sitting is no different from a canine "Please."

To train your dog, you need gentle hands, a loving heart and a good attitude.

Also, include numerous short training interludes during every enjoyable canine pastime, for example, when playing with the dog or when she is running in the park. In this fashion, doggy distractions may be effectively converted into rewards for training. Just as all games have rules, fun becomes training . . . and training becomes fun.

Eventually, rewards actually become unnecessary to continue motivating your dog. If trained with consideration and kindness, performing the desired behaviors will become self-rewarding and, in a sense, your dog will motivate herself. Just as it is not necessary to reward a human companion during an enjoyable walk in the park, or following a game of tennis, it is hardly necessary to reward our best friend—the dog—for walking by our side or while playing fetch. Human company during enjoyable activities is reward enough for most dogs.

Even though your dog has become self-motivating, it's still good to praise and pet her a lot and offer rewards once in a while, especially for a good job well done. And if for no other reason, praising and rewarding others is good for the human heart.

PUNISHMENT

Without a doubt, lure-reward training is by far the best way to teach: Entice your dog to do what you want and then reward her for doing so. Unfortunately, a human shortcoming is to take the good for granted and to moan and groan at the bad. Specifically, the dog's many good behaviors are ignored while the owner focuses on punishing the dog for making mistakes. In extreme cases, instruction is *limited* to punishing mistakes made by a trainee dog, child, employee or husband, even though it has been proven punishment training is notoriously inefficient and ineffective and is decidedly unfriendly and combative. It teaches the dog that training is a drag, almost as quickly as it teaches the dog to dislike her trainer. Why treat our best friends like our worst enemies?

Punishment training is also much more laborious and time consuming. Whereas it takes only a finite amount of time to teach a dog what to chew, for example, it takes much, much longer to punish the dog for each and every mistake. Remember, *there is only one right way!* So why not teach that right way from the outset?!

To make matters worse, punishment training causes severe lapses in the dog's reliability. Since it is obviously impossible to punish the dog each and every time she misbehaves, the dog quickly learns to distinguish between those times when she must comply (so as to avoid impending punishment) and those times when she need not comply, because punishment is impossible. Such times include when the dog is off leash and 6 feet away, when the owner is otherwise engaged (talking to a friend, watching television, taking a shower, tending to the baby or chatting on the telephone) or when the dog is left at home alone.

Instances of misbehavior will be numerous when the owner is away, because even when the dog complied in the owner's looming presence, she did so unwillingly. The dog was forced to act against her will, rather than molding her will to want to please. Hence, when the owner is absent, not only does the dog know she need not comply, she simply does not want to. Again, the trainee is not a stubborn vindictive beast, but rather the trainer has failed to teach. Punishment training invariably creates unpredictable Jekyll and Hyde behavior.

Trainer's Tools

Many training books extol the virtues of a vast array of training paraphernalia and electronic and metallic gizmos, most of which are designed for canine restraint, correction and punishment, rather than for actual facilitation of doggy education. In reality, most effective training tools are not found in stores; they come from within ourselves. In addition to a willing dog, all you really need is a functional human brain, gentle hands, a loving heart and a good attitude.

In terms of equipment, all dogs do require a quality buckle collar to sport dog tags and to attach the leash (for safety and to comply with local leash laws). Hollow chew toys (like Kongs or sterilized longbones) and a dog bed or collapsible crate are musts for housetraining. Three additional tools are required:

1. specific lures (training treats and toys) to predict and prompt specific desired behaviors;

2. rewards (praise, affection, training treats and toys) to reinforce for the dog what a lot of fun it all is; and

3. knowledge—how to convert the dog's favorite activities and games (potential distractions to training) into "life-rewards," which may be employed to facilitate training.

The most powerful of these is *knowledge*. Education is the key! Watch training classes, participate in training classes, watch videos, read books, enjoy play-training with your dog and then your dog will say "Please," and your dog will say "Thank you!"

Housetraining

If dogs were left to their own devices, certainly they would chew, dig and bark for entertainment and then no doubt highlight a few areas of their living space with sprinkles of urine, in much the same way we decorate by hanging pictures. Consequently, when we ask a dog to live with us, we must teach her *where* she may dig, *where* she may perform her toilet duties, *what* she may chew and *when* she may bark. After all, when left at home alone for many hours, we cannot expect the dog to amuse herself by completing crosswords or watching the soaps on TV!

Also, it would be decidedly unfair to keep the house rules a secret from the dog, and then get angry and punish the poor critter for inevitably transgressing rules she did not even know existed. Remember: Without adequate education and guidance, the dog will be forced to establish her own rules—doggy rules—and most probably will be at odds with the owner's view of domestic living.

Since most problems develop during the first few days the dog is at home, prospective dog owners must be certain they are quite clear about the principles of housetraining *before* they get a dog. Early misbehaviors quickly become established as the *status quo*—

105

becoming firmly entrenched as hard-to-break bad habits, which set the precedent for years to come. Make sure to teach your dog good habits right from the start. Good habits are just as hard to break as bad ones!

Ideally, when a new dog comes home, try to arrange for someone to be present as much as possible during the first few days (for adult dogs) or weeks for puppies. With only a little forethought, it is surprisingly easy to find a puppy sitter, such as a retired person, who would be willing to eat from your refrigerator and watch your television while keeping an eye on the newcomer to encourage the dog to play with chew toys and to ensure she goes outside on a regular basis.

POTTY TRAINING

To teach the dog where to relieve herself:

1. never let her make a single mistake;
2. let her know where you want her to go; and
3. handsomely reward her for doing so: "GOOOOOOOD DOG!!!" liver treat, liver treat, liver treat!

Preventing Mistakes

A single mistake is a training disaster, since it heralds many more in future weeks. And each time the dog soils the house, this further reinforces the dog's unfortunate preference for an indoor, carpeted toilet. *Do not let an unhousetrained dog have full run of the house.*

When you are away from home, or cannot pay full attention, confine the dog to an area where elimination is appropriate, such as an outdoor run or, better still, a small, comfortable indoor kennel with access to an outdoor run. When confined in this manner, most dogs will naturally housetrain themselves.

If that's not possible, confine the dog to an area, such as a utility room, kitchen, basement or garage, where elimination may not be desired in the long run but as an interim measure it is certainly preferable to doing it all around the house. Use newspaper to cover the floor of the dog's day room. The newspaper may be used to soak up the urine and to wrap up and dispose of the feces. Once your dog develops a pre-ferred spot for eliminating, it is only necessary to cover that part of the floor with newspaper. The smaller pa-pered area may then be moved (only a little each day) towards the door to the outside. Thus the dog will develop the tendency to go to the door when she needs to relieve herself.

Never confine an unhouse-trained dog to a crate for long periods. Doing so would force the dog to soil the crate and ruin its usefulness as an aid for housetraining (see the following discussion).

Teaching Where

In order to teach your dog where you would like her to do her business, you have to be there to direct the proceedings—an obvious, yet often neglected, fact of life. In order to be there to teach the dog *where* to go, you need to know *when* she needs to go. Indeed, the success of housetrain-ing depends on the owner's ability to predict these times. Certainly, a regular feeding schedule will facil-itate prediction somewhat, but there is nothing like "loading the deck" and influencing the timing of the outcome yourself!

Whenever you are at home, make sure the dog is under constant supervision and/or confined to a small

The first few weeks at home are the most important and influential in your dog's life.

area. If already well trained, simply instruct the dog to lie down in her bed or basket. Alternatively, confine the dog to a crate (doggy den) or tie-down (a short, 18-inch lead that can be clipped to an eye hook in the baseboard near her bed). Short-term close confinement strongly inhibits urination and defecation, since the dog does not want to soil her sleeping area. Thus, when you release the puppydog each hour, she will definitely need to urinate immediately and defecate every third or fourth hour. Keep the dog confined to her doggy den and take her to her intended toilet area each hour, every hour and on the hour.

When taking your dog outside, instruct her to sit quietly before opening the door—she will soon learn to sit by the door when she needs to go out!

Teaching Why

Being able to predict when the dog needs to go enables the owner to be on the spot to praise and reward the dog. Each hour, hurry the dog to the intended toilet area in the yard, issue the appropriate instruction ("Go pee!" or "Go poop!"), then give the dog three to four minutes to produce. Praise and offer a couple of training treats when successful. The treats are important because many people fail to praise their dogs with feeling . . . and housetraining is hardly the time for understatement. So either loosen up and enthusiastically praise that dog: "Wuzzzer-wuzzer-wuzzer, hoooser good wuffer den? Hoooo went pee for Daddy?" Or say "Good dog!" as best you can and offer the treats for effect.

Following elimination is an ideal time for a spot of play-training in the yard or house. Also, an empty dog may be allowed greater freedom around the house for the next half hour or so, just as long as you keep an eye out to make sure she does not get into other kinds of mischief. If you are preoccupied and cannot pay full attention, confine the dog to her doggy den once more to enjoy a peaceful snooze or to play with her many chew toys.

If your dog does not eliminate within the allotted time outside—no biggie! Back to her doggy den, and then try again after another hour.

As I own large dogs, I always feel more relaxed walking an empty dog, knowing that I will not need to finish our stroll weighted down with bags of feces!

Beware of falling into the trap of walking the dog to get her to eliminate. The good ol' dog walk is such an enormous highlight in the dog's life that it represents the single biggest potential reward in domestic dogdom. However, when in a hurry, or during inclement weather, many owners abruptly terminate the walk the moment the dog has done her business. This, in effect, severely punishes the dog for doing the right thing, in the right place at the right time. Consequently, many dogs become strongly inhibited from eliminating outdoors because they know it will signal an abrupt end to an otherwise thoroughly enjoyable walk.

Instead, instruct the dog to relieve herself in the yard prior to going for a walk. If you follow the above instructions, most dogs soon learn to eliminate on cue. As soon as the dog eliminates, praise (and offer a treat or two)—"Good dog! Let's go walkies!" Use the walk as a reward for eliminating in the yard. If the dog does not go, put her back in her doggy den and think about a walk later on. You will find with a "No feces—no walk" policy, your dog will become one of the fastest defecators in the business.

If you do not have a backyard, instruct the dog to eliminate right outside your front door prior to the walk. Not only will this facilitate clean up and disposal of the feces in your own trash can but, also, the walk may again be used as a colossal reward.

CHEWING AND BARKING

Short-term close confinement also teaches the dog that occasional quiet moments are a reality of domestic living. Your puppydog is extremely impressionable during her first few weeks at home. Regular confinement at this time soon exerts a calming influence over the dog's personality. Remember, once the dog is housetrained and calmer, there will be a whole lifetime ahead for the dog to enjoy full run of the house and garden. On the other hand, by letting the newcomer have unrestricted access to the entire household and allowing her to run willy-nilly, she will most certainly develop a bunch of behavior problems in short order, no doubt necessitating confinement later in life. It would not be fair to remedially restrain and confine a dog you have trained, through neglect, to run free.

When confining the dog, make sure she always has an impressive array of suitable chew toys. Kongs and sterilized longbones (both readily available from pet stores) make the best chew toys, since they are hollow and may be stuffed with treats to heighten the dog's interest. For example, by stuffing the little hole at the top of a Kong with a small piece of freeze-dried liver, the dog will not want to leave it alone.

Remember, treats do not have to be junk food and they certainly should not represent extra calories. Rather, treats should be part of each dog's regular

Make sure your puppy has suitable chew toys.

daily diet: Some food may be served in the dog's bowl for breakfast and dinner, some food may be used as training treats, and some food may be used for stuffing chew toys. I regularly stuff my dogs' many Kongs with different shaped biscuits and kibble. The kibble seems to fall out fairly easily, as do the oval-shaped biscuits, thus rewarding the dog instantaneously for checking out the chew toys. The bone-shaped biscuits fall out after a while, rewarding the dog for worrying at the chew toy. But the triangular biscuits never come out. They remain inside the Kong as lures, maintaining the dog's fascination with her chew toy. To further focus the dog's interest, I always make sure to flavor the triangular biscuits by rubbing them with a little cheese or freeze-dried liver.

To teach come, call your dog, open your arms as a welcoming signal, wave a toy or a treat and praise for every step in your direction.

If stuffed chew toys are reserved especially for times the dog is confined, the puppydog will soon learn to enjoy quiet moments in her doggy den and she will quickly develop a chew-toy habit— a good habit! This is a simple *autoshaping* process; all the owner has to do is set up the situation and the dog all but trains herself— easy and effective. Even when the dog is given run of the house, her first inclination will be to indulge her rewarding chew-toy habit rather than destroy less-attractive household articles, such as curtains, carpets, chairs and compact disks. Similarly, a chew-toy chewer will be less inclined to scratch and chew herself excessively. Also, if the dog busies herself as a recreational chewer, she will be less inclined to develop into a recreational barker or digger when left at home alone.

Stuff a number of chew toys whenever the dog is left confined and remove the extra-special-tasting treats when you return. Your dog will now amuse herself with her chew toys before falling asleep and then resume playing with her chew toys when she expects you to return. Since most owner-absent misbehavior happens right after you leave and right before your expected return, your puppydog will now be conveniently preoccupied with her chew toys at these times.

Come and Sit

Most puppies will happily approach virtually anyone, whether called or not; that is, until they collide with adolescence and

develop other more important doggy interests, such as sniffing a multiplicity of exquisite odors on the grass. Your mission, Mr./Ms. Owner, is to teach and reward the pup for coming reliably, willingly and happily when called—and you have just three months to get it done. Unless adequately reinforced, your puppy's tendency to approach people will self-destruct by adolescence.

Call your dog ("Tina, come!"), open your arms (and maybe squat down) as a welcoming signal, waggle a treat or toy as a lure and reward the puppydog when she comes running. Do not wait to praise the dog until she reaches you—she may come 95 percent of the way and then run off after some distraction. Instead, praise the dog's *first* step towards you and continue praising enthusiastically for *every* step she takes in your direction.

When the rapidly approaching puppy dog is three lengths away from impact, instruct her to sit ("Tina, sit!") and hold the lure in front of you in an outstretched hand to prevent her from hitting you midchest and knocking you flat on your back! As Tina decelerates to nose the lure, move the treat upwards and backwards just over her muzzle with an upwards motion of your extended arm (palm-upwards). As the dog looks up to follow the lure, she will sit down (if she jumps up, you are holding the lure too high). Praise the dog for sitting. Move backwards and call her again. Repeat this many times over, always praising when Tina comes and sits; on occasion, reward her.

For the first couple of trials, use a training treat both as a lure to entice the dog to come and sit and as a reward for doing so. Thereafter, try to use different items as lures and rewards. For example, lure the dog with a Kong or Frisbee but reward her with a food treat. Or lure the dog with a food treat but pat her and throw a tennis ball as a reward. After just a few repetitions, dispense with the lures and rewards; the dog will begin to respond willingly to your verbal requests and hand signals just for the prospect of praise from your heart and affection from your hands.

Instruct every family member, friend and visitor how to get the dog to come and sit. Invite people over for a series of pooch parties; do not keep the pup a secret—let other people enjoy this puppy, and let the pup enjoy other people. Puppydog parties are not only fun, they easily attract a lot of people to help *you* train *your* dog. Unless you teach your dog how to meet people, that is, to sit for greetings, no doubt the dog will resort to jumping up. Then you and the visitors will get annoyed, and the dog will be punished. This is not fair. *Send out those invitations for puppy parties and teach your dog to be mannerly and socially acceptable.*

Even though your dog quickly masters obedient recalls in the house, her reliability may falter when playing in the backyard or local park. Ironically, it is *the owner* who has unintentionally trained the dog *not* to respond in these instances. By allowing the dog to play and run around and otherwise have a good time, but then to call the dog to put her on leash to take her home, the dog quickly learns playing is fun but training is a drag. Thus, playing in the park becomes a severe distraction, which works against training. Bad news!

Instead, whether playing with the dog off leash or on leash, request her to come at frequent intervals—say, every minute or so. On most occasions, praise and pet the dog for a few seconds while she is sitting, then tell her to go play again. For especially fast recalls, offer a couple of training treats and take the time to praise and pet the dog enthusiastically before releasing her. The dog will learn that coming when called is not necessarily the end of the play session, and neither is it the end of the world; rather, it signals an enjoyable, quality time-out with the owner before resuming play once more. In fact, playing in the park now becomes a very effective life-reward, which works to facilitate training by reinforcing each obedient and timely recall. Good news!

Sit, Down, Stand and Rollover

Teaching the dog a variety of body positions is easy for owner and dog, impressive for spectators and extremely useful for all. Using lure-reward techniques, it is possible to train several positions at once to verbal commands or hand signals (which impress the socks off onlookers).

Sit and ***down***—the two control commands—prevent or resolve nearly a hundred behavior problems. For example, if the dog happily and obediently sits or lies down when requested, she cannot jump on visitors, dash out the front door, run around and chase her tail, pester other dogs, harass cats or annoy family, friends or strangers. Additionally, "Sit" or "Down" are the best emergency commands for off-leash control.

It is easier to teach and maintain a reliable sit than maintain a reliable recall. *Sit* is the purest and simplest of commands—either the dog is sitting or she is not. If there is any change of circumstances or potential danger in the park, for example, simply instruct the dog to sit. If she sits, you have a number of options: Allow the dog to resume playing when she is safe, walk up and put the dog on leash or call the dog. The dog will be much more likely to come when called if she has already acknowledged her compliance by sitting. If the dog does not sit in the park—train her to!

Stand and ***rollover-stay*** are the two positions for examining the dog. Your veterinarian will love you to distraction if you take a little time to teach the dog to stand still and roll over and play possum. Also, your vet bills will be smaller because it will take the veterinarian less time to examine your dog. The rollover-stay is an especially useful command and is really just a variation of the down-stay: Whereas the dog lies prone in the traditional down, she lies supine in the rollover-stay.

As with teaching come and sit, the training techniques to teach the dog to assume all other body positions on cue are user-friendly and dog-friendly. Simply give the appropriate request, lure the dog into the desired body position using a training treat or toy and then *praise* (and maybe reward) the dog as soon as she complies. Try not to touch the dog to get her to respond. If you teach the dog by guiding her into position, the dog will quickly learn that rump-pressure means sit, for example, but as yet you still have no control over your dog if she is just 6 feet away. It will still be necessary to teach the dog to sit on request. So do not make training a time-consuming two-step process; instead, teach the dog to sit to a verbal request or hand signal from the outset. Once the dog sits willingly when requested, by all means use your hands to pet the dog when she does so.

To teach *down* when the dog is already sitting, say "Tina, down!," hold the lure in one hand (palm down) and lower that hand to the floor between the dog's forepaws. As the dog lowers her head to follow the lure, slowly move the lure away from the dog just a fraction (in front of her paws). The dog will lie down as she stretches her nose forward to follow the lure. Praise the dog when she does so. If the dog stands up, you pulled the lure away too far and too quickly.

When teaching the dog to lie down from the standing position, say "Down" and lower the lure to the floor as before. Once the dog has lowered her forequarters and assumed a play bow, gently and slowly move the lure *towards* the dog between her forelegs. Praise the dog as soon as her rear end plops down.

After just a couple of trials it will be possible to alternate sits and downs and have the dog energetically perform doggy push-ups. Praise the dog a lot, and after half a dozen or so push-ups reward the dog with a training treat or toy. You will notice the more energetically you move your arm—upwards (palm up) to get the dog to sit, and downwards (palm down) to get the dog to lie down—the more energetically the dog responds to your requests. Now try training the dog in silence and you will notice she has also learned to respond to hand signals. Yeah! Not too shabby for the first session.

To teach *stand* from the sitting position, say "Tina, stand," slowly move the lure half a dog-length away from the dog's nose, keeping it at nose level, and praise the dog as she stands to follow the lure. As soon

Using a food lure to teach sit, down and stand. 1) "Phoenix, sit." 2) Hand palm upwards, move lure up and back over dog's muzzle. 3) "Good sit, Phoenix!" 4) "Phoenix, down." 5) Hand palm downwards, move lure down to lie between dog's forepaws. 6) "Phoenix, off. Good down, Phoenix!" 7) "Phoenix, sit!" 8) Palm upwards, move lure up and back, keeping it close to dog's muzzle. 9) "Good sit, Phoenix!"

10) "Phoenix, stand!" 11) Move lure away from dog at nose height, then lower it a tad. 12) "Phoenix, off! Good stand, Phoenix!" 13) "Phoenix, down!" 14) Hand palm downwards, move lure down to lie between dog's forepaws. 15) "Phoenix, off! Good down-stay, Phoenix!" 16) "Phoenix, stand!" 17) Move lure away from dog's muzzle up to nose height. 18) "Phoenix, off! Good stand-stay, Phoenix. Now we'll make the vet and groomer happy!"

as the dog stands, lower the lure to just beneath the dog's chin to entice her to look down; otherwise she will stand and then sit immediately. To prompt the dog to stand from the down position, move the lure half a dog-length upwards and away from the dog, holding the lure at standing nose height from the floor.

Teaching *rollover* is best started from the down position, with the dog lying on one side, or at least with both hind legs stretched out on the same side. Say "Tina, bang!" and move the lure backwards and alongside the dog's muzzle to her elbow (on the side of her outstretched hind legs). Once the dog looks to the side and backwards, very slowly move the lure upwards to the dog's shoulder and backbone. Tickling the dog in the goolies (groin area) often invokes a reflex-raising of the hind leg as an appeasement gesture, which facilitates the tendency to roll over. If you move the lure too quickly and the dog jumps into the standing position, have patience and start again. As soon as the dog rolls onto her back, keep the lure stationary and mesmerize the dog with a relaxing tummy rub.

To teach *rollover-stay* when the dog is standing or moving, say "Tina, bang!" and give the appropriate hand signal (with index finger pointed and thumb cocked in true Sam Spade fashion), then in one fluid movement lure her to first lie down and then rollover-stay as above.

Teaching the dog to *stay* in each of the above four positions becomes a piece of cake after first teaching the dog not to worry at the toy or treat training lure. This is best accomplished by hand feeding dinner kibble. Hold a piece of kibble firmly in your hand and softly instruct "Off!" Ignore any licking and slobbering *for however long the dog worries at the treat,* but say "Take it!" and offer the kibble *the instant* the dog breaks contact with her muzzle. Repeat this a few times, and then up the ante and insist the dog remove her muzzle for one whole second before offering the kibble. Then progressively refine your criteria and have the dog not touch your hand (or treat) for longer and longer periods on each trial, such as for two seconds, four seconds, then six, ten, fifteen, twenty, thirty seconds and so on.

The dog soon learns: (1) worrying at the treat never gets results, whereas (2) noncontact is often rewarded after a variable time lapse.

Teaching *"Off!"* has many useful applications in its own right. Additionally, instructing the dog not to touch a training lure often produces spontaneous and magical stays. Request the dog to stand-stay, for example, and not to touch the lure. At first set your sights on a short two-second stay before rewarding the dog. (Remember, every long journey begins with a single step.) However, on subsequent trials, gradually and progressively increase the length of stay required to receive a reward. In no time at all your dog will stand calmly for a minute or so.

Relevancy Training

Once you have taught the dog what you expect her to do when requested to come, sit, lie down, stand, roll-over and stay, the time is right to teach the dog *why* she should comply with your wishes. The secret is to have many (*many*) extremely short training interludes (two to five seconds each) at numerous (*numerous*) times during the course of the dog's day. Especially work with the dog immediately *before* the dog's good times and *during* the dog's good times. For example, ask your dog to sit and/or lie down each time before opening doors, serving meals, offering treats and tummy rubs; ask the dog to perform a few controlled doggy push-ups before letting her off leash or throwing a tennis ball; and perhaps request the dog to sit-down-sit-stand-down-stand-rollover before inviting her to cuddle on the couch.

Similarly, request the dog to sit many times during play or on walks, and in no time at all the dog will be only too pleased to follow your instructions because she has learned that a compliant response heralds all sorts of goodies. Basically all you are trying to teach the dog is how to say please: "Please throw the tennis ball. Please may I snuggle on the couch."

Remember, it is important to keep training interludes short and to have many short sessions each and every day. The shortest (and most useful) session comprises asking the dog to sit and then go play during a play session. When trained this way, your dog will soon associate training with good times. In fact, the dog may be unable to distinguish between training and good times and, indeed, there should be no distinction. The warped concept that training involves forcing the dog to comply and/or dominating her will is totally at odds with the picture of a truly well-trained dog. In reality, enjoying a game of training with a dog is no different from enjoying a game of backgammon or tennis with a friend; and walking with a dog should be no different from strolling with a spouse, or with buddies on the golf course.

Walk by Your Side

Many people attempt to teach a dog to heel by putting her on a leash and physically correcting the dog when she makes mistakes. There are a number of things seriously wrong with this approach, the first being that most people do not want precision heeling; rather, they simply want the dog to follow or walk by their side. Second, when physically restrained during "training," even though the dog may grudgingly mope by your side when "handcuffed" on leash, let's see what happens when she is off leash. History! The dog is in the next county because she never enjoyed walking with you on leash and you have no control over her off leash. So let's just teach the dog off leash from the outset to *want* to walk with us. Third, if the dog has not been trained to heel, it is a trifle hasty to think about punishing the poor dog for making mistakes and breaking heeling rules she didn't even know existed. This is simply not fair! Surely, if the dog had been adequately taught how to heel, she would seldom make mistakes and hence there would be no need to correct the dog. Remember, each mistake and each correction (punishment) advertise the trainer's inadequacy, not the dog's. The dog is not stubborn, she is not stupid and she is not bad. Even if she were, she would still require training, so let's train her properly.

Let's teach the dog to *enjoy* following us and to *want* to walk by our side off leash. Then it will be easier to teach high-precision off-leash heeling patterns if desired. Before going on outdoor walks, it is necessary to teach the dog not to pull. Then it becomes easy to teach on-leash walking and heeling because the dog already wants to walk with you, she is familiar with the desired walking and heeling positions and she knows not to pull.

FOLLOWING

Start by training your dog to follow you. Many puppies will follow if you simply walk away from them and maybe click your fingers or chuckle. Adult dogs may require additional enticement to stimulate them to follow, such as a training lure or, at the very least, a lively trainer. To teach the dog to follow: (1) keep walking and (2) walk away from the dog. If the dog attempts to lead or lag, change pace; slow down if the dog forges too far ahead, but speed up if she lags too far behind. Say "Steady!" or "Easy!" each time before you slow down and "Quickly!" or "Hustle!" each time before you speed up, and the dog will learn to change pace on cue. If the dog lags or leads too far, or if she wanders right or left, simply walk quickly in the opposite direction and maybe even run away from the dog and hide.

Practicing is a lot of fun; you can set up a course in your home, yard or park to do this. Indoors, entice the dog to follow upstairs, into a bedroom, into the bathroom, downstairs, around the living room couch, zigzagging between dining room chairs and into the kitchen for dinner. Outdoors, get the dog to follow around park benches, trees, shrubs and along walkways and lines in the grass. (For safety outdoors, it is advisable to attach a long line on the dog, but never exert corrective tension on the line.)

Remember, following has a lot to do with attitude—
your attitude! Most probably your dog will *not* want to
follow Mr. Grumpy Troll with the personality of wilted
lettuce. Lighten up—walk with a jaunty step, whistle a
happy tune, sing, skip and tell jokes to your dog and
she will be right there by your side.

BY YOUR SIDE

It is smart to train the dog to walk close on one side or
the other—either side will do, your choice. When walking, jogging or cycling, it is generally bad news to have
the dog suddenly cut in front of you. In fact, I train my
dogs to walk "By my side" and "Other side"—both very
useful instructions. It is possible to position the dog
fairly accurately by looking to the appropriate side and
clicking your fingers or slapping your thigh on that
side. A precise positioning may be attained by holding
a training lure, such as a chew toy, tennis ball or food
treat. Stop and stand still several times throughout the
walk, just as you would when window shopping or
meeting a friend. Use the lure to make sure the dog
slows down and stays close whenever you stop.

When teaching the dog to heel, we generally want
her to sit in heel position when we stop. Teach heel

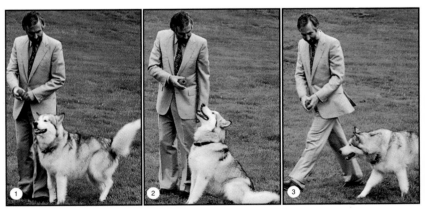

Using a toy to teach sit-heel-sit sequences: 1) "Phoenix, sit!" Standing still, move lure up and back over dog's muzzle . . . 2) to position dog sitting in heel position on your left side. 3) Say "Phoenix, heel!" and walk ahead, wagging lure in left hand. Change lure to right hand in preparation for sit signal. Say "Sit" and then . . .

position at the standstill and the dog will learn that the default heel position is sitting by your side (left or right—your choice, unless you wish to compete in obedience trials, in which case the dog must heel on the left).

Several times a day, stand up and call your dog to come and sit in heel position—"Tina, heel!" For example, instruct the dog to come to heel each time there are commercials on TV, or each time you turn a page of a novel, and the dog will get it in a single evening.

Practice straight-line heeling and turns separately. With the dog sitting at heel, teach her to turn in place. After each quarter-turn, half-turn or full turn in place, lure the dog to sit at heel. Now it's time for short straight-line heeling sequences, no more than a few steps at a time. Always think of heeling in terms of sit-heel-sit sequences—start and end with the dog in position and do your best to keep her there when moving. Progressively increase the number of steps in each sequence. When the dog remains close for 20 yards of straight-line heeling, it is time to add a few turns and then sign up for a happy-heeling obedience class to get some advice from the experts.

4) use hand signal to lure dog to sit as you stop. Eventually, dog will sit automatically at heel whenever you stop. 5) "Good dog!"

No Pulling on Leash

You can start teaching your dog not to pull on leash anywhere—in front of the television or outdoors—but regardless of location, you must not take a single step with tension in the leash. For a reason known only to dogs, even just a couple of paces of pulling on leash is intrinsically motivating and diabolically rewarding. Instead, attach the leash to the dog's collar, grasp the other end firmly with both hands held close to your chest, and stand still—do not budge an inch. Have somebody watch you with a stopwatch to time your progress, or else you will never believe this will work and so you will not even try the exercise, and your shoulder and the dog's neck will be traumatized for years to come.

Stand still and wait for the dog to stop pulling, and to sit and/or lie down. All dogs stop pulling and sit eventually. Most take only a couple of minutes; the all-time record is 22½ minutes. Time how long it takes. Gently praise the dog when she stops pulling, and as soon as she sits, enthusiastically praise the dog and take just one step forward, then immediately stand still. This single step usually demonstrates the ballistic reinforcing nature of pulling on leash; most dogs explode to the end of the leash, so be prepared for the strain. Stand firm and wait for the dog to sit again. Repeat this half a dozen times and you will probably notice a progressive reduction in the force of the dog's one-step explosions and a radical reduction in the time it takes for the dog to sit each time.

As the dog learns "Sit we go" and "Pull we stop," she will begin to walk forward calmly with each single step and automatically sit when you stop. Now try two steps before you stop. Wooooooo! Scary! When the dog has mastered two steps at a time, try for three. After each success, progressively increase the number of steps in the sequence: try four steps and then six, eight, ten and twenty steps before stopping. Congratulations! You are now walking the dog on leash.

Whenever walking with the dog (off leash or on leash), make sure you stop periodically to practice a few position commands and stays before instructing the dog to "Walk on!" (Remember, you want the dog to be compliant everywhere, not just in the kitchen when her dinner is at hand.) For example, stopping every 25 yards to briefly train the dog amounts to over 200 training interludes within a single 3-mile stroll. And each training session is in a different location. You will not believe the improvement within just the first mile of the first walk.

To put it another way, integrating training into a walk offers 200 separate opportunities to use the continuance of the walk as a reward to reinforce the dog's education. Moreover, some training interludes may comprise continuing education for the dog's walking skills: Alternate short periods of the dog walking calmly by your side with periods when the dog is allowed to sniff and investigate the environment. Now sniffing odors on the grass and meeting other dogs become rewards which reinforce the dog's calm and mannerly demeanor. Good Lord! Whatever next? Many enjoyable walks together of course. Happy trails!

THE IMPORTANCE OF TRICKS

Nothing will improve a dog's quality of life better than having a few tricks under her belt. Teaching any trick expands the dog's vocabulary, which facilitates communication and improves the owner's control. Also, specific tricks help prevent and resolve specific behavior problems. For example, by teaching the dog to fetch her toys, the dog learns carrying a toy makes the owner happy and, therefore, will be more likely to chew her toy than other inappropriate items.

More important, teaching tricks prompts owners to lighten up and train with a sunny disposition. Really, tricks should be no different from any other behaviors we put on cue. But they are. When teaching tricks, owners have a much sweeter attitude, which in turn motivates the dog and improves her willingness to comply. The dog feels tricks are a blast, but formal commands are a drag. In fact, tricks are so enjoyable, they may be used as rewards in training by asking the dog to come, sit and down-stay and then rollover for a tummy rub. Go on, try it: Crack a smile and even giggle when the dog promptly and willingly lies down and stays.

Most important, performing tricks prompts onlookers to smile and giggle. Many people are scared of dogs, especially large ones. And nothing can be more off-putting for a dog than to be constantly confronted by strangers who don't like her because of her size or the way she looks. Uneasy people put the dog on edge, causing her to back off and bark, only frightening people all the more. And so a vicious circle develops, with the people's fear fueling the dog's fear *and vice versa*. Instead, tie a pink ribbon to your dog's collar and practice all sorts of tricks on walks and in the park, and you will be pleasantly amazed how it changes people's attitudes toward your friendly dog. The dog's repertoire of tricks is limited only by the trainer's imagination. Below I have described three of my favorites:

SPEAK AND SHUSH

The training sequence involved in teaching a dog to bark on request is no different from that used when training any behavior on cue: request—lure—response—reward. As always, the secret of success lies in finding an effective lure. If the dog always barks at the doorbell, for example, say "Rover, speak!", have an accomplice ring the doorbell, then reward the dog for barking. After a few woofs, ask Rover to "Shush!", waggle a food treat under her nose (to entice her to sniff and thus to shush), praise her when quiet and eventually offer the treat as a reward. Alternate "Speak" and "Shush," progressively increasing the length of shush-time between each barking bout.

PLAY BOW

With the dog standing, say "Bow!" and lower the food lure (palm upwards) to rest between the dog's forepaws. Praise as the dog lowers her forequarters and sternum to the ground (as when teaching the down), but then lure the dog to stand and offer the treat. On successive trials, gradually increase the length of time the dog is required to remain in the play bow posture in order to gain a food reward. If the dog's rear end collapses into a down, say nothing and offer no reward; simply start over.

BE A BEAR

With the dog sitting backed into a corner to prevent her from toppling over backwards, say "Be a bear!" With bent paw and palm down, raise a lure upwards and backwards along the top of the dog's muzzle. Praise the dog when she sits up on her haunches and offer the treat as a reward. To prevent the dog from standing on her hind legs, keep the lure closer to the dog's muzzle. On each trial, progressively increase the length of time the dog is required to sit up to receive a food reward. Since lure-reward training is so easy, teach the dog to stand and walk on her hind legs as well!

Teaching "Be a Bear"

chapter 9

Getting
Active
with your Dog

by Bardi McLennan

Once you and your dog have graduated from basic obedience training and are beginning to work together as a team, you can take part in the growing world of dog activities. There are so many fun things to do with your dog! Just remember, people and dogs don't always learn at the same pace, so don't be upset if you (or your dog) need more than two basic training courses before your team becomes operational. Even smart dogs don't go straight to college from kindergarten!

Just as there are events geared to certain types of dogs, so there are ones that are more appealing to certain types of people. In some activities, you give the commands and your dog does the work (upland game hunting is one example), while in others, such as agility, you'll both get a workout. You may want to aim for prestigious titles to add to your dog's name, or you may want nothing more than the sheer enjoyment of being around other people and their dogs. Passive or active, participation has its own rewards.

Consider your dog's physical capabilities when looking into any of the canine activities. It's easy to see that a Basset Hound is not built for the racetrack, nor would a Chihuahua be the breed of choice for pulling a sled. A loyal dog will attempt almost anything you ask him to do, so it is up to you to know your dog's limitations. A dog must be physically sound in order to compete at any level in athletic activities, and being mentally sound is a definite plus. Advanced age, however, may not be a deterrent. Many dogs still hunt and herd at ten or twelve years of age. It's entirely possible for dogs to be "fit at 50." Take your dog for a checkup, explain to your vet the type of activity you have in mind and be guided by his or her findings.

All dogs seem to love playing flyball.

You needn't be restricted to breed-specific sports if it's only fun you're after. Certain AKC activities are limited to designated breeds; however, as each new trial, test or sport has grown in popularity, so has the variety of breeds encouraged to participate at a fun level.

But don't shortchange your fun, or that of your dog, by thinking only of the basic function of her breed. Once a dog has learned how to learn, she can be taught to do just about anything as long as the size of the dog is right for the job and you both think it is fun and rewarding. In other words, you are a team.

To get involved in any of the activities detailed in this chapter, look for the names and addresses of the organizations that sponsor them in Chapter 13. You can also ask your breeder or a local dog trainer for contacts.

You can compete in obedience trials with a well trained dog.

Official American Kennel Club Activities

The following tests and trials are some of the events sanctioned by the AKC and sponsored by various dog clubs. Your dog's expertise will be rewarded with impressive titles. You can participate just for fun, or be competitive and go for those awards.

OBEDIENCE

Training classes begin with pups as young as three months of age in kindergarten puppy training, then advance to pre-novice (all exercises on lead) and go on to novice, which is where you'll start off-lead work. In obedience classes dogs learn to sit, stay, heel and come through a variety of exercises. Once you've got the basics down, you can enter obedience trials and work toward earning your dog's first degree, a C.D. (Companion Dog).

The next level is called "Open," in which jumps and retrieves perk up the dog's interest. Passing grades in competition at this level earn a C.D.X. (Companion Dog Excellent). Beyond that lies the goal of the most ambitious—Utility (U.D. and even U.D.X. or OTCh, an Obedience Champion).

AGILITY

All dogs can participate in the latest canine sport to have gained worldwide popularity for its fun and excitement, agility. It began in England as a canine version of horse show-jumping, but because dogs are more agile and able to perform on verbal commands, extra feats were added such as climbing, balancing and racing through tunnels or in and out of weave poles.

Many of the obstacles (regulation or homemade) can be set up in your own backyard. If the agility bug bites, you could end up in international competition!

For starters, your dog should be obedience trained, even though, in the beginning, the lessons may all be taught on lead. Once the dog understands the commands (and you do, too), it's as easy as guiding the dog over a prescribed course, one obstacle at a time. In competition, the race is against the clock, so wear your running shoes! The dog starts with 200 points and the judge deducts for infractions and misadventures along the way.

All dogs seem to love agility and respond to it as if they were being turned loose in a playground paradise. Your dog's enthusiasm will be contagious; agility turns into great fun for dog and owner.

FIELD TRIALS AND HUNTING TESTS

There are field trials and hunting tests for the sporting breeds—retrievers, spaniels and pointing breeds, and for some hounds—Bassets, Beagles and Dachshunds. Field trials are competitive events that test a dog's ability to perform the functions for which she was bred. Hunting tests, which are open to retrievers,

---

TITLES AWARDED BY THE AKC

Conformation: Ch. (Champion)

Obedience: CD (Companion Dog); CDX (Companion Dog Excellent); UD (Utility Dog); UDX (Utility Dog Excellent); OTCh. (Obedience Trial Champion)

Field: JH (Junior Hunter); SH (Senior Hunter); MH (Master Hunter); AFCh. (Amateur Field Champion); FCh. (Field Champion)

Lure Coursing: JC (Junior Courser); SC (Senior Courser)

Herding: HT (Herding Tested); PT (Pre-Trial Tested); HS (Herding Started); HI (Herding Intermediate); HX (Herding Excellent); HCh. (Herding Champion)

Tracking: TD (Tracking Dog); TDX (Tracking Dog Excellent)

Agility: NAD (Novice Agility); OAD (Open Agility); ADX (Agility Excellent); MAX (Master Agility)

Earthdog Tests: JE (Junior Earthdog); SE (Senior Earthdog); ME (Master Earthdog)

Canine Good Citizen: CGC

Combination: DC (Dual Champion—Ch. and Fch.); TC (Triple Champion—Ch., Fch., and OTCh.)

spaniels and pointing breeds only, are noncompetitive and are a means of judging the dog's ability as well as that of the handler.

Hunting is a very large and complex part of canine sports, and if you own one of the breeds that hunts, the events are a great treat for your dog and you. He gets to do what he was bred for, and you get to work with him and watch him do it. You'll be proud of and amazed at what your dog can do.

Fortunately, the AKC publishes a series of booklets on these events, which outline the rules and regulations and include a glossary of the sometimes complicated terms. The AKC also publishes newsletters for field trialers and hunting test enthusiasts. The United Kennel Club (UKC) also has informative materials for the hunter and his dog.

Retrievers and other sporting breeds get to do what they're bred to in hunting tests.

HERDING TESTS AND TRIALS

Herding, like hunting, dates back to the first known uses man made of dogs. The interest in herding today is widespread, and if you own a herding breed, you can join in the activity. Herding dogs are tested for their natural skills to keep a flock of ducks, sheep or cattle together. If your dog shows potential, you can start at the testing level, where your dog can earn a title for showing an inherent herding ability. With training you can advance to the trial level, where your dog should be capable of controlling even difficult livestock in diverse situations.

LURE COURSING

The AKC Tests and Trials for Lure Coursing are open to traditional sighthounds—Greyhounds, Whippets,

Borzoi, Salukis, Afghan Hounds, Ibizan Hounds and Scottish Deerhounds—as well as to Basenjis and Rhodesian Ridgebacks. Hounds are judged on overall ability, follow, speed, agility and endurance. This is possibly the most exciting of the trials for spectators, because the speed and agility of the dogs is awesome to watch as they chase the lure (or "course") in heats of two or three dogs at a time.

TRACKING

Tracking is another activity in which almost any dog can compete because every dog that sniffs the ground when taken outdoors is, in fact, tracking. The hard part comes when the rules as to what, when and where the dog tracks are determined by a person, not the dog! Tracking tests cover a large area of fields, woods and roads. The tracks are

laid hours before the dogs go to work on them, and include "tricks" like cross-tracks and sharp turns. If you're interested in search-and-rescue work, this is the place to start.

This tracking dog is hot on the trail.

EARTHDOG TESTS FOR SMALL TERRIERS AND DACHSHUNDS

These tests are open to Australian, Bedlington, Border, Cairn, Dandie Dinmont, Smooth and Wire Fox, Lakeland, Norfolk, Norwich, Scottish, Sealyham, Skye, Welsh and West Highland White Terriers as well as Dachshunds. The dogs need no prior training for this terrier sport. There is a qualifying test on the day of the event, so dog and handler learn the rules on the spot. These tests, or "digs," sometimes end with informal races in the late afternoon.

Here are some of the extracurricular obedience and racing activities that are not regulated by the AKC or UKC, but are generally run by clubs or a group of dog fanciers and are often open to all.

Canine Freestyle This activity is something new on the scene and is variously likened to dancing, dressage or ice skating. It is meant to show the athleticism of the dog, but also requires showmanship on the part of the dog's handler. If you and your dog like to ham it up for friends, you might want to look into freestyle.

Lure coursing lets sighthounds do what they do best—run!

Scent Hurdle Racing Scent hurdle racing is purely a fun activity sponsored by obedience clubs with members forming competing teams. The height of the hurdles is based on the size of the shortest dog on the team. On a signal, one team dog is released on each of two side-by-side courses and must clear every hurdle before picking up its own dumbbell from a platform and returning over the jumps to the handler. As each dog returns, the next on that team is sent. Of course, that is what the dogs are supposed to do. When the dogs improvise (going under or around the hurdles, stealing another dog's dumbbell, and so forth), it no doubt frustrates the handlers, but just adds to the fun for everyone else.

Flyball This type of racing is similar, but after negotiating the four hurdles, the dog comes to a flyball box, steps on a lever that releases a tennis ball into the air, catches the ball and returns over the hurdles to the starting point. This game also becomes extremely fun for spectators because the dogs sometimes cheat by catching a ball released by the dog in the next lane. Three titles can be earned—Flyball Dog (F.D.), Flyball Dog Excellent (F.D.X.) and Flyball Dog Champion (Fb.D.Ch.)—all awarded by the North American Flyball Association, Inc.

Dogsledding The name conjures up the Rocky Mountains or the frigid North, but you can find dogsled clubs in such unlikely spots as Maryland, North Carolina and Virginia! Dogsledding is primarily for the Nordic breeds such as the Alaskan Malamutes, Siberian Huskies and Samoyeds, but other breeds can try. There are some practical backyard applications to this sport, too. With parental supervision, almost any strong dog could pull a child's sled.

Coming over the A-frame on an agility course.

These are just some of the many recreational ways you can get to know and understand your multifaceted dog better and have fun doing it.

chapter 10

Your Dog
and your
Family

by Bardi McLennan

Adding a dog automatically increases your family by one, no matter whether you live alone in an apartment or are part of a mother, father and six kids household. The single-person family is fair game for numerous and varied canine misconceptions as to who is dog and who pays the bills, whereas a dog in a houseful of children will consider himself to be just one of the gang, littermates all. One dog and one child may give a dog reason to believe they are both kids or both dogs.

Either interpretation requires parental supervision and sometimes speedy intervention.

As soon as one paw goes through the door into your home, Rufus (or Rufina) has to make many adjustments to become a part of your family. Your job is to make him fit in as painlessly as possible. An older dog may have some frame of reference from past experience, but to a 10-week-old puppy, everything is brand new: people, furniture, stairs, when and where people eat, sleep or watch TV, his own place and everyone else's space, smells, sounds, outdoors—everything!

Puppies, and newly acquired dogs of any age, do not need what we think of as "freedom." If you leave a new dog or puppy loose in the house, you will almost certainly return to chaotic destruction and the dog will forever after equate your homecoming with a time of punishment to be dreaded. It is unfair to give your dog what amounts to "freedom to get into trouble." Instead, confine him to a crate for brief periods of your absence (up to three or four hours) and, for the long haul, a workday for example, confine him to one untrashable area with his own toys, a bowl of water and a radio left on (low) in another room.

Lots of pets get along with each other just fine.

For the first few days, when not confined, put Rufus on a long leash tied to your wrist or waist. This umbilical cord method enables the dog to learn all about you from your body language and voice, and to learn by his own actions which things in the house are NO! and which ones are rewarded by "Good dog." Housetraining will be easier with the pup always by your side. Speaking of which, accidents do happen. That goal of "completely housetrained" takes up to a year, or the length of time it takes the pup to mature.

The All-Adult Family

Most dogs in an adults-only household today are likely to be latchkey pets, with no one home all day but the dog. When you return after a tough day on the job, the dog can and should be your relaxation therapy. But going home can instead be a daily frustration.

Separation anxiety is a very common problem for the dog in a working household. It may begin with whines and barks of loneliness, but it will soon escalate into a frenzied destruction derby. That is why it is so important to set aside the time to teach a dog to relax when left alone in his confined area and to understand that he can trust you to return.

Let the dog get used to your work schedule in easy stages. Confine him to one room and go in and out of that room over and over again. Be casual about it. No physical, voice or eye contact. When the pup no longer even notices your comings and goings, leave the house for varying lengths of time, returning to stay home for a few minutes and gradually increasing the time away. This training can take days, but the dog is learning that you haven't left him forever and that he can trust you.

Any time you leave the dog, but especially during this training period, be casual about your departure. No anxiety-building fond farewells. Just "Bye" and go! Remember the "Good dog" when you return to find everything more or less as you left it.

If things are a mess (or even a disaster) when you return, greet the dog, take him outside to eliminate, and then put him in his crate while you clean up. Rant and rave in the shower! *Do not* punish the dog. You were not there when it happened, and the rule is: Only punish as you catch the dog in the act of wrongdoing. Obviously, it makes sense to get your latchkey puppy when you'll have a week or two to spend on these training essentials.

Family weekend activities should include Rufus whenever possible. Depending on the pup's age, now is the time for a long walk in the park, playtime in the backyard, a hike in the woods. Socializing is as important as health care, good food and physical exercise, so visiting Aunt Emma or Uncle Harry and the next-door neighbor's dog or cat is essential to developing an outgoing, friendly temperament in your pet.

If you are a single adult, socializing Rufus at home and away will prevent him from becoming overly protective of you (or just overly attached) and will also prevent such behavioral problems as dominance or fear of strangers.

Babies

Whether already here or on the way, babies figure larger than life in the eyes of a dog. If the dog is there first, let him in on all your baby preparations in the house. When baby arrives, let Rufus sniff any item of clothing that has been on the baby before Junior comes home. Then let Mom greet the dog first before introducing the new family member. Hold the baby down for the dog to see and sniff, but make sure someone's holding the dog on lead in case of any sudden moves. Don't play keep-away or tease the dog with the baby, which only invites undesirable jumping up.

The dog and the baby are "family," and for starters can be treated almost as equals. Things rapidly change, however, especially when baby takes to creeping around on all fours on the dog's turf or, better yet, has yummy pudding all over her face and hands! That's when a lot of things in the dog's and baby's lives become more separate than equal.

Dogs are perfect confidants.

Toddlers make terrible dog owners, but if you can't avoid the combination, use patient discipline (that is, positive teaching rather than punishment), and use time-outs before you run out of patience.

A dog and a baby (or toddler, or an assertive young child) should never be left alone together. Take the dog with you or confine him. With a baby or youngsters in the house, you'll have plenty of use for that wonderful canine safety device called a crate!

Young Children

Any dog in a house with kids will behave pretty much as the kids do, good or bad. But even good dogs and good children can get into trouble when play becomes rowdy and active.

Teach children how to play nicely with a puppy.

Legs bobbing up and down, shrill voices screeching, a ball hurtling overhead, all add up to exuberant frustration for a dog who's just trying to be part of the gang. In a pack of puppies, any legs or toys being chased would be caught by a set of teeth, and all the pups involved would understand that is how the game is played. Kids do not understand this, nor do parents tolerate it. Bring Rufus indoors before you have reason to regret it. This is time-out, not a punishment.

You can explain the situation to the children and tell them they must play quieter games until the puppy learns not to grab them with his mouth. Unfortunately, you can't explain it that easily to the dog. With adult supervision, they will learn how to play together.

Young children love to tease. Sticking their faces or wiggling their hands or fingers in the dog's face is teasing. To another person it might be just annoying, but it is threatening to a dog. There's another difference: We can make the child stop by an explanation, but the only way a dog can stop it is with a warning growl and then with teeth. Teasing is the major cause of children being bitten by their pets. Treat it seriously.

Older Children

The best age for a child to get a first dog is between the ages of 8 and 12. That's when kids are able to accept some real responsibility for their pet. Even so, take the child's vow of "I will never *ever* forget to feed (brush, walk, etc.) the dog" for what it's worth: a child's good intention at that moment. Most kids today have extra lessons, soccer practice, Little League, ballet, and so forth piled on top of school schedules. There will be many times when Mom will have to come to the dog's rescue. "I walked the dog for you so you can set the table for me" is one way to get around a missed appointment without laying on blame or guilt.

Kids in this age group make excellent obedience trainers because they are into the teaching/learning process themselves and they lack the self-consciousness of adults. Attending a dog show is something the whole family can enjoy, and watching Junior Showmanship may catch the eye of the kids. Older children can begin to get involved in many of the recreational activities that were reviewed in the previous chapter. Some of the agility obstacles, for example, can be set up in the backyard as a family project (with an adult making sure all the equipment is safe and secure for the dog).

Older kids are also beginning to look to the future, and may envision themselves as veterinarians or trainers or show dog handlers or writers of the next Lassie best-seller. Dogs are perfect confidants for these dreams. They won't tell a soul.

Other Pets

Introduce all pets tactfully. In a dog/cat situation, hold the dog, not the cat. Let two dogs meet on neutral turf—a stroll in the park or a walk down the street—with both on loose leads to permit all the normal canine ways of saying hello, including routine sniffing, circling, more sniffing, and so on. Small creatures such as hamsters, chinchillas or mice must be kept safe from their natural predators (dogs and cats).

Festive Family Occasions

Parties are great for people, but not necessarily for puppies. Until all the guests have arrived, put the dog in his crate or in a room where he won't be disturbed. A socialized dog can join the fun later as long as he's not underfoot, annoying guests or into the hors d'oeuvres.

There are a few dangers to consider, too. Doors opening and closing can allow a puppy to slip out unnoticed in the confusion, and you'll be organizing a search party instead of playing host or hostess. Party food and buffet service are not for dogs. Let Rufus party in his crate with a nice big dog biscuit.

At Christmas time, not only are tree decorations dangerous and breakable (and perhaps family heirlooms), but extreme caution should be taken with the lights, cords and outlets for the tree lights and any other festive lighting. Occasionally a dog lifts a leg, ignoring the fact that the tree is indoors. To avoid this, use a canine repellent, made for gardens, on the tree. Or keep him out of the tree room unless supervised. And whatever you do, *don't* invite trouble by hanging his toys on the tree!

Car Travel

Before you plan a vacation by car or RV with Rufus, be sure he enjoys car travel. Nothing spoils a holiday quicker than a carsick dog! Work within the dog's comfort level. Get in the car with the dog in his crate or attached to a canine car safety belt and just sit there until he relaxes. That's all. Next time, get in the car, turn on the engine and go nowhere. Just sit. When that is okay, turn on the engine and go around the block. Now you can go for a ride and include a stop where you get out, leaving the dog for a minute or two.

On a warm day, always park in the shade and leave windows open several inches. And return quickly. It only takes 10 minutes for a car to become an overheated steel death trap.

Motel or Pet Motel?

Not all motels or hotels accept pets, but you have a much better choice today than even a few years ago. To find a dog-friendly lodging, look at *On the Road Again With Man's Best Friend,* a series of directories that detail bed and breakfasts, inns, family resorts and other hotels/motels. Some places require a refundable deposit to cover any damage incurred by the dog. More B&Bs accept pets now, but some restrict the size.

If taking Rufus with you is not feasible, check out boarding kennels in your area. Your veterinarian may offer this service, or recommend a kennel or two he or she is familiar with. Go see the facilities for yourself, ask about exercise, diet, housing, and so on. Or, if you'd rather have Rufus stay home, look into bonded petsitters, many of whom will also bring in the mail and water your plants.

chapter 11

Your Dog
and your
Community

by Bardi McLennan

Step outside your home with your dog and you are no longer just family, you are both part of your community. This is when the phrase "responsible pet ownership" takes on serious implications. For starters, it means you pick up after your dog—not just occasionally, but every time your dog eliminates away from home. That means you have joined the Plastic Baggy Brigade! You always have plastic sandwich bags in your pocket and several in the car. It means you teach your kids how to use them, too. If you think this is "yucky," just imagine what the person (a non-doggy person) who inadvertently steps in the mess thinks!

Your responsibility extends to your neighbors: To their ears (no annoying barking); to their property (their garbage, their lawn, their flower beds, their cat—especially their cat); to their kids (on bikes, at play); to their kids' toys and sports equipment.

There are numerous dog-related laws, ranging from simple dog licensing and leash laws to those holding you liable for any physical injury or property damage done by your dog. These laws are in place to protect everyone in the community, including you and your dog. There are town ordinances and state laws which are by no means the same in all towns or all states. Ignorance of the law won't get you off the hook. The time to find out what the laws are where you live is now.

Be sure your dog's license is current. This is not just a good local ordinance, it can make the difference between finding your lost dog or not. Many states now require proof of rabies vaccination and that the dog has been spayed or neutered before issuing a license. At the same time, keep up the dog's annual immunizations.

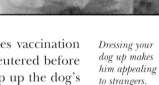

Dressing your dog up makes him appealing to strangers.

Never let your dog run loose in the neighborhood. This will not only keep you on the right side of the leash law, it's the outdoor version of the rule about not giving your dog "freedom to get into trouble."

Good Canine Citizen

Sometimes it's hard for a dog's owner to assess whether or not the dog is sufficiently socialized to be accepted by the community at large. Does Rufus or Rufina display good, controlled behavior in public? The AKC's Canine Good Citizen program is available through many dog organizations. If your dog passes the test, the title "CGC" is earned.

The overall purpose is to turn your dog into a good neighbor and to teach you about your responsibility to your community as a dog owner. Here are the ten things your dog must do willingly:

1. Accept a stranger stopping to chat with you.
2. Sit and be petted by a stranger.
3. Allow a stranger to handle him or her as a groomer or veterinarian would.
4. Walk nicely on a loose lead.
5. Walk calmly through a crowd.
6. Sit and down on command, then stay in a sit or down position while you walk away.
7. Come when called.
8. Casually greet another dog.
9. React confidently to distractions.
10. Accept being left alone with someone other than you and not become overly agitated or nervous.

Schools and Dogs

Schools are getting involved with pet ownership on an educational level. It has been proven that children who are kind to animals are humane in their attitude toward other people as adults.

A dog is a child's best friend, and so children are often primary pet owners, if not the primary caregivers. Unfortunately, they are also the ones most often bitten by dogs. This occurs due to a lack of understanding that pets, no matter how sweet, cuddly and loving, are still animals. Schools, along with parents, dog clubs, dog fanciers and the AKC, are working to change all that with video programs for children not only in grade school, but in the nursery school and pre-kindergarten age group. Teaching youngsters how to be responsible dog owners is important community work. When your dog has a CGC, volunteer to take part in an educational classroom event put on by your dog club.

Boy Scout Merit Badge

A Merit Badge for Dog Care can be earned by any Boy Scout ages 11 to 18. The requirements are not easy, but amount to a complete course in responsible dog care and general ownership. Here are just a few of the things a Scout must do to earn that badge:

> Point out ten parts of the dog using the correct names.

> Give a report (signed by parent or guardian) on your care of the dog (feeding, food used, housing, exercising, grooming and bathing), plus what has been done to keep the dog healthy.

> Explain the right way to obedience train a dog, and demonstrate three comments.

> Several of the requirements have to do with health care, including first aid, handling a hurt dog, and the dangers of home treatment for a serious ailment.

> The final requirement is to know the local laws and ordinances involving dogs.

There are similar programs for Girl Scouts and 4-H members.

Local Clubs

Local dog clubs are no longer in existence just to put on a yearly dog show. Today, they are apt to be the hub of the community's involvement with pets. Dog clubs conduct educational forums with big-name speakers, stage demonstrations of canine talent in a busy mall and take dogs of various breeds to schools for class-room discussion.

The quickest way to feel accepted as a member in a club is to volunteer your services! Offer to help with something—anything—and watch your popularity (and your interest) grow.

Therapy Dogs

Once your dog has earned that essential CGC and reliably demonstrates a steady, calm temperament, you could look into what therapy dogs are doing in your area.

Therapy dogs go with their owners to visit patients at hospitals or nursing homes, generally remaining on leash but able to coax a pat from a stiffened hand, a smile from a blank face, a few words from sealed lips or a hug from someone in need of love.

Nursing homes cover a wide range of patient care. Some specialize in care of the elderly, some in the treatment of specific illnesses, some in physical therapy. Children's facilities also welcome visits from trained therapy dogs for boosting morale in their pediatric patients. Hospice care for the terminally ill and the at-home care of AIDS patients are other areas where this canine visiting is desperately needed. Therapy dog training comes first.

Your dog can make a difference in lots of lives.

There is a lot more involved than just taking your nice friendly pooch to someone's bedside. Doing therapy dog work involves your own emotional stability as well as that of your dog. But once you have met all the requirements for this work, making the rounds once a week or once a month with your therapy dog is possibly the most rewarding of all community activities.

Disaster Aid

This community service is definitely not for everyone, partly because it is time-consuming. The initial training is rigorous, and there can be no let-up in the continuing workouts, because members are on call 24 hours a day to go wherever they are needed at a

148

moment's notice. But if you think you would like to be able to assist in a disaster, look into search-and-rescue work. The network of search-and-rescue volunteers is worldwide, and all members of the American Rescue Dog Association (ARDA) who are qualified to do this work are volunteers who train and maintain their own dogs.

Physical Aid

Most people are familiar with Seeing Eye dogs, which serve as blind people's eyes, but not with all the other work that dogs are trained to do to assist the disabled. Dogs are also specially trained to pull wheelchairs, carry school books, pick up dropped objects, open and close doors. Some also are ears for the deaf. All these assistance-trained dogs, by the way, are allowed anywhere "No Pet" signs exist (as are therapy dogs when properly identified). Getting started in any of this fascinating work requires a background in dog training and canine behavior, but there are also volunteer jobs ranging from answering the phone to cleaning out kennels to providing a foster home for a puppy. You have only to ask.

Making the rounds with your therapy dog can be very rewarding.

149

part four

Beyond the Basics

chapter 12

Recommended Reading

Books

ABOUT HEALTH CARE

Ackerman, Lowell. *Guide to Skin and Haircoat Problems in Dogs.* Loveland, Colo.: Alpine Publications, 1994.

Alderton, David. *The Dog Care Manual.* Hauppauge, N.Y.: Barron's Educational Series, Inc., 1986.

American Kennel Club. *American Kennel Club Dog Care and Training.* New York: Howell Book House, 1991.

Bamberger, Michelle, DVM. *Help! The Quick Guide to First Aid for Your Dog.* New York: Howell Book House, 1995.

Carlson, Delbert, DVM, and James Giffin, MD. *Dog Owner's Home Veterinary Handbook.* New York: Howell Book House, 1992.

DeBitetto, James, DVM, and Sarah Hodgson. *You & Your Puppy.* New York: Howell Book House, 1995.

Humphries, Jim, DVM. *Dr. Jim's Animal Clinic for Dogs.* New York: Howell Book House, 1994.

McGinnis, Terri. *The Well Dog Book.* New York: Random House, 1991.

Pitcairn, Richard and Susan. *Natural Health for Dogs.* Emmaus, Pa.: Rodale Press, 1982.

ABOUT DOG SHOWS

Hall, Lynn. *Dog Showing for Beginners.* New York: Howell Book House, 1994.

Nichols, Virginia Tuck. *How to Show Your Own Dog.* Neptune, N. J.: TFH, 1970.

Vanacore, Connie. *Dog Showing, An Owner's Guide.* New York: Howell Book House, 1990.

ABOUT TRAINING

Ammen, Amy. *Training in No Time*. New York: Howell Book House, 1995.

Baer, Ted. *Communicating With Your Dog*. Hauppauge, N.Y.: Barron's Educational Series, Inc., 1989.

Benjamin, Carol Lea. *Dog Problems*. New York: Howell Book House, 1989.

Benjamin, Carol Lea. *Dog Training for Kids*. New York: Howell Book House, 1988.

Benjamin, Carol Lea. *Mother Knows Best*. New York: Howell Book House, 1985.

Benjamin, Carol Lea. *Surviving Your Dog's Adolescence*. New York: Howell Book House, 1993.

Bohnenkamp, Gwen. *Manners for the Modern Dog*. San Francisco: Perfect Paws, 1990.

Dibra, Bashkim. *Dog Training by Bash*. New York: Dell, 1992.

Dunbar, Ian, PhD, MRCVS. *Dr. Dunbar's Good Little Dog Book*, James & Kenneth Publishers, 2140 Shattuck Ave. #2406, Berkeley, Calif. 94704. (510) 658–8588. Order from the publisher.

Dunbar, Ian, PhD, MRCVS. *How to Teach a New Dog Old Tricks*, James & Kenneth Publishers. Order from the publisher; address above.

Dunbar, Ian, PhD, MRCVS, and Gwen Bohnenkamp. Booklets on *Preventing Aggression; Housetraining; Chewing; Digging; Barking; Socialization; Fearfulness; and Fighting*, James & Kenneth Publishers. Order from the publisher; address above.

Evans, Job Michael. *People, Pooches and Problems*. New York: Howell Book House, 1991.

Kilcommons, Brian and Sarah Wilson. *Good Owners, Great Dogs*. New York: Warner Books, 1992.

McMains, Joel M. *Dog Logic—Companion Obedience*. New York: Howell Book House, 1992.

Rutherford, Clarice and David H. Neil, MRCVS. *How to Raise a Puppy You Can Live With*. Loveland, Colo.: Alpine Publications, 1982.

Volhard, Jack and Melissa Bartlett. *What All Good Dogs Should Know: The Sensible Way to Train*. New York: Howell Book House, 1991.

ABOUT BREEDING

Harris, Beth J. Finder. *Breeding a Litter, The Complete Book of Prenatal and Postnatal Care*. New York: Howell Book House, 1983.

Holst, Phyllis, DVM. *Canine Reproduction*. Loveland, Colo.: Alpine Publications, 1985.

Walkowicz, Chris and Bonnie Wilcox, DVM. *Successful Dog Breeding, The Complete Handbook of Canine Midwifery.* New York: Howell Book House, 1994.

ABOUT ACTIVITIES

American Rescue Dog Association. *Search and Rescue Dogs.* New York: Howell Book House, 1991.

Barwig, Susan and Stewart Hilliard. *Schutzhund.* New York: Howell Book House, 1991.

Beaman, Arthur S. *Lure Coursing.* New York: Howell Book House, 1994.

Daniels, Julie. *Enjoying Dog Agility—From Backyard to Competition.* New York: Doral Publishing, 1990.

Davis, Kathy Diamond. *Therapy Dogs.* New York: Howell Book House, 1992.

Gallup, Davis Anne. *Running With Man's Best Friend.* Loveland, Colo.: Alpine Publications, 1986.

Habgood, Dawn and Robert. *On the Road Again With Man's Best Friend.* New England, Mid-Atlantic, West Coast and Southeast editions. Selective guides to area bed and breakfasts, inns, hotels and resorts that welcome guests and their dogs. New York: Howell Book House, 1995.

Holland, Vergil S. *Herding Dogs.* New York: Howell Book House, 1994.

LaBelle, Charlene G. *Backpacking With Your Dog.* Loveland, Colo.: Alpine Publications, 1993.

Simmons-Moake, Jane. *Agility Training, The Fun Sport for All Dogs.* New York: Howell Book House, 1991.

Spencer, James B. *Hup! Training Flushing Spaniels the American Way.* New York: Howell Book House, 1992.

Spencer, James B. *Point! Training the All-Seasons Birddog.* New York: Howell Book House, 1995.

Tarrant, Bill. *Training the Hunting Retriever.* New York: Howell Book House, 1991.

Volhard, Jack and Wendy. *The Canine Good Citizen.* New York: Howell Book House, 1994.

General Titles

Haggerty, Captain Arthur J. *How to Get Your Pet Into Show Business.* New York: Howell Book House, 1994.

McLennan, Bardi. *Dogs and Kids, Parenting Tips.* New York: Howell Book House, 1993.

Moran, Patti J. *Pet Sitting for Profit, A Complete Manual for Professional Success.* New York: Howell Book House, 1992.

Scalisi, Danny and Libby Moses. *When Rover Just Won't Do, Over 2,000 Suggestions for Naming Your Dog*. New York: Howell Book House, 1993.

Sife, Wallace, PhD. *The Loss of a Pet*. New York: Howell Book House, 1993.

Wrede, Barbara J. *Civilizing Your Puppy*. Hauppauge, N.Y.: Barron's Educational Series, 1992.

Magazines

The AKC GAZETTE, The Official Journal for the Sport of Purebred Dogs. American Kennel Club, 51 Madison Ave., New York, NY.

Bloodlines Journal. United Kennel Club, 100 E. Kilgore Rd., Kalamazoo, MI.

Dog Fancy. Fancy Publications, 3 Burroughs, Irvine, CA 92718

Dog World. Maclean Hunter Publishing Corp., 29 N. Wacker Dr., Chicago, IL 60606.

Videos

"SIRIUS Puppy Training," by Ian Dunbar, PhD, MRCVS. James & Kenneth Publishers, 2140 Shattuck Ave. #2406, Berkeley, CA 94704. Order from the publisher.

"Training the Companion Dog," from Dr. Dunbar's British TV Series, James & Kenneth Publishers. (See address above).

The American Kennel Club produces videos on every breed of dog, as well as on hunting tests, field trials and other areas of interest to purebred dog owners. For more information, write to AKC/Video Fulfillment, 5580 Centerview Dr., Suite 200, Raleigh, NC 27606.

chapter 13

Resources

Breed Clubs

Every breed recognized by the American Kennel Club has a national (parent) club. National clubs are a great source of information on your breed. You can get the name of the secretary of the club by contacting:

The American Kennel Club
51 Madison Avenue
New York, NY 10010
(212) 696-8200

There are also numerous all-breed, individual breed, obedience, hunting and other special-interest dog clubs across the country. The American Kennel Club can provide you with a geographical list of clubs to find ones in your area. Contact them at the above address.

Registry Organizations

Registry organizations register purebred dogs. The American Kennel Club is the oldest and largest in this country, and currently recognizes over 130 breeds. The United Kennel Club registers some breeds the AKC doesn't (including the American Pit Bull Terrier and the Miniature Fox Terrier) as well as many of the same breeds. The others included here are for your reference; the AKC can provide you with a list of foreign registries.

American Kennel Club
51 Madison Avenue
New York, NY 10010

United Kennel Club (UKC)
100 E. Kilgore Road
Kalamazoo, MI 49001-5598

American Dog Breeders Assn.
P.O. Box 1771
Salt Lake City, UT 84110
(Registers American Pit Bull Terriers)

Canadian Kennel Club
89 Skyway Avenue
Etobicoke, Ontario
Canada M9W 6R4

National Stock Dog Registry
P.O. Box 402
Butler, IN 46721
(Registers working stock dogs)

Orthopedic Foundation for Animals (OFA)
2300 E. Nifong Blvd.
Columbia, MO 65201-3856
(Hip registry)

Activity Clubs
Write to these organizations for information on the
activities they sponsor.

American Kennel Club
51 Madison Avenue
New York, NY 10010
(Conformation Shows, Obedience Trials, Field
Trials and Hunting Tests, Agility, Canine Good

Citizen, Lure Coursing, Herding, Tracking, Earthdog Tests, Coonhunting.)

United Kennel Club
100 E. Kilgore Road
Kalamazoo, MI 49001-5598
(Conformation Shows, Obedience Trials, Agility, Hunting for Various Breeds, Terrier Trials and more.)

North American Flyball Assn.
1342 Jeff St.
Ypsilanti, MI 48198

International Sled Dog Racing Assn.
P.O. Box 446
Norman, ID 83848-0446

North American Working Dog Assn., Inc.
Southeast Kreisgruppe
P.O. Box 833
Brunswick, GA 31521

Trainers

Association of Pet Dog Trainers
P.O. Box 385
Davis, CA 95617
(800) PET–DOGS

American Dog Trainers' Network
161 West 4th St.
New York, NY 10014
(212) 727–7257

National Association of Dog Obedience Instructors
2286 East Steel Rd.
St. Johns, MI 48879

Associations

American Dog Owners Assn.
1654 Columbia Tpk.
Castleton, NY 12033
(Combats anti-dog legislation)

Delta Society
P.O. Box 1080
Renton, WA 98057-1080
(Promotes the human/animal bond through
pet-assisted therapy and other programs)

Dog Writers Assn. of America (DWAA)
Sally Cooper, Secy.
222 Woodchuck Ln.
Harwinton, CT 06791

National Assn. for Search and Rescue (NASAR)
P.O. Box 3709
Fairfax, VA 22038

Therapy Dogs International
6 Hilltop Road
Mendham, NJ 07945